WALKING
WITH GOD

Richard Baxter

Vintage Puritan Series
GLH PUBLISHING
Louisville, Kentucky

Sourced from *The Description, Reasons, and Reward of the Believer's Walking with God.*
Published by J. Owen, 13, Little Bell Alley; London: 1825.

ISBN-13: 978-1-941129-26-5

CONTENTS

CHAPTER I.

Being to speak of our Converse with God in Solitude, I think it will not be unsuitable, nor unserviceable to the ends of that discourse, if I here premise a short description of the General Duty of Practical Godliness, as it is called in Scripture 'a Walking with God.' It is here commended to us in the example of holy Enoch, whose excellency is recorded in this signal character, that "he walked with God:" and his special reward expressed in the words following, "and he was not, for God took him." I shall speak most of his character, and then somewhat of his reward.

The Samaritan and vulgar Latin versions do strictly translate the Hebrew as we read it: but the interpretation of the Septuagint, the Syriac, the Chaldee, and the Arabic, are rather good expositions (all set together) of the meaning of the word, than strict translations. The Septuagint and Syriac read it, 'Enoch pleased God.' The Chaldee hath, 'Enoch walked in the fear of God.' And the Arabic, 'he walked in obedience to God.' And indeed to walk in the fear and obedience of God, and thereby to please him, is the principal thing in our "walking with God." The same character is given of Noah, in Gen. vi. 19. and the extraordinary reward annexed; he and his family were saved in the deluge. And the holy life which God commanded Abraham, is called 'a walking before God.' "Walk before me, and be thou perfect;" (Gen. xvii. 1.) And in the New Testament the Christian conversation is ordinarily called by the name of Walking. Sometimes a 'walking in Christ;' as Col. ii. 6. Sometimes a 'walking in the Spirit, in which we live.' (Gal. v. 25.) And a 'walking after the Spirit.' (Rom. viii. 1.) Sometimes a 'walking in the light, as God is in the light.' (1 John i. 7.) Those that 'abide in Christ must so walk even as he hath walked.' (1 John ii. 6.) These phrases set together tell us, what it is to walk with God. But I think it not unprofitable somewhat more particularly to show you what this walking with God doth contain.

As atheism is the sum of wickedness, so all true religiousness is called by the name of Godliness or Holiness, which is nothing else but our devotedness to God, and living to him, and our relation to him as thus devoted in heart and life. Practical atheism is a "living as without God in the world." (Ephes. ii. 12.) Godliness is contrary to practical atheism, and is a living as with and to God in the world and in the church, and is here called a walking with God. And it containeth in it these particulars.

1. To walk with God includeth the practical acknowledgment (that is made by the will as well as the understanding) of the grand attributes of God, and his relations to man; that he is Infinite in his Being, that is, Immense and Eternal; as also in his Power, Wisdom and Goodness. That he is the Creator, Redeemer and Sanctifier. That he is our absolute Lord (or Owner), our most righteous Governor, and most bountiful Benefactor (or Father). That "of him, and through him, and to him, are all things:" That "in him we live, and move, and have our being:" That he is the fountain, or first cause, from which all (proper) being, truth and goodness in the creature is but a derived stream. To have the soul unfeignedly resign itself to

1

him, as his own; and subject itself to him as our Governor, walking in the awe of his sovereign power; sensible of the strong obligation of his laws, which reason, justice and necessity do all command us to obey. To live as in full dependence on him: to have the first and greatest respect unto him: a more observant respect to him than to our rulers: a more obedient respect to him than to our masters: a more dependent, tender, and honourable respect to him than to parents, or our nearest friends. Thus "he that cometh to God" (as God, and so as to be accepted of him), "must believe that he is," (his essential attributes) and (what he is in his relations to man; especially that as our Governor and Benefactor) "he is the Rewarder of them that diligently seek him." (Heb. xi. 6.) The impress of a Deity in his essential and relative attributes must be upon the heart of him that walks with God. Yea, the being of God must be much more remarkable to him, than the being of all creatures, and his presence more regarded, than the presence of the creature; and all things must be to us in comparison of God, as a candle is in comparison of the sun. His greatness and transcendent excellencies must so overpower them all, as to make them less observed and regarded, by his taking up our chief observation and regard.

2. Our walking with God includeth our reconciliation to him, and that we are not in our natural state of enmity, but made his children and friends in Christ. "Can two walk together unless they be agreed?" (Amos iii. 3.) Enmity is against unity; disaffection causeth aversion, and flying from each other: yea, the fears of a guilty child may make him fly from his father's presence, till there be a particular reconciliation, besides the general state of reconciliation. A provoking, faulty child doth dwell with God his Father, though under the continual terror of his frowns; but to walk with him (in the full sense) is more than to be related to him, and to dwell with him. In a large sense indeed all God's children may be said to walk with him, as it signifieth only a conversation ordered in godliness, sincerity and simplicity. But in this more sublime sense, as it signifieth a lively exercise of faith and love, and heavenly-mindedness, and a course of complacential contemplation, and holy converse with God, so it is proper only to some of the sounder and more vigilant industrious believers. And hereto it is necessary, not only that we be justified and reconciled to God from our state of enmity, but also that we be pardoned, justified and reconciled from our particular wounding falls, which are more than the ordinary infirmities of believers. And also it is necessary that we have grateful, friendly thoughts of God: that we have so much sense of his excellency, goodness and kindness to ourselves, as may give us a complacency in conversing with him, and may make the thoughts and mention of him to be desirable and pleasing to us. Walking with God doth import, though not the full assurance of his special love and grace to us, yet such an apprehension of his love and goodness, as may draw the heart to think of him with desire, if not with delight. A loathness to draw near him, to think of him, or to mention him, a weariness of his special service, are contrary to this special walking with God.

3. Our walking with God, doth include our esteeming and intending Him as the ultimate end and felicity of our souls. He is not to be sought, or loved, or conversed with, as a means to any greater good (for there is no greater), nor as inferior, or merely equal unto any. His goodness must be the most powerful attractive of our love: his favour must be valued as our happiness; and the pleasing of him must be our most industrious employment. To walk with him, is to live in the warming, reviving sunshine of his goodness, and to feel a delighting, satisfying virtue in his love and gracious presence. To live as those that are not their own,

and that have their lives, and faculties, and provisions, and helps for their master's service: as a horse or dog is of so much worth, as he is of use to him that owneth him; and that is the best that is the most serviceable to his master: yet with this very great difference, that man being a more noble and capacious creature, is admitted not only into a state of service, but of sonship, and friendship, and communion with God; and is allowed and appointed to share more in the pleasure and fruits of his services, and to put in his own felicity and delight into his end; not only because self-love is natural and necessary to the creature, but also because he is under the promise of a reward; and (more than either) because he is a lover, and not only a servant, and his work is principally a work of love, and therefore his end is 'finis amantis,' the end of a lover, which is mutual complacency in the exercises of love.

He that seeketh not first the kingdom and righteousness of God, and referreth not other things to him, but seeks first the creature, and God only for it, doth but deny God in his heart, and basely subject him to the works of his own hands, and doth not walk with God, but vilify and reject him. If you live not to God, even to obey, and please, and honour him, you do not walk with him; but walk contrary to him (by living to his enemies, the flesh, the world, and the devil), and therefore God will "walk contrary to you." (Levit. xxvi. 21, 23, 24, 27, 28.) You were both created and redeemed, though for your own felicity, yet principally for the glory and pleasure of your Creator and Redeemer; and for no felicity of your own, but what consisteth in pleasing him, glorifying him, and enjoying him: "Whether therefore we eat, or drink, or whatever we do, it should all be done to the glory of God." (1 Cor. x. 31.) He that regardeth a day, or regardeth it not; he that eateth, or that eateth not, must do it to the Lord. (And though a good intention will not sanctify a forbidden action, yet sins of ignorance and mere frailty are forborne and pardoned of God, when it is his glory and service that is sincerely intended, though there be a mistake in the choice of means.) "None of us liveth to himself, and no man dieth to himself: for whether we live, we live unto the Lord; and whether we die, we die unto the Lord. Whether we live therefore or die, we are the Lord's. For to this end Christ both died, rose, and revived, that he might be Lord both of the dead and living." (Rom. xiv. 6-9.) Our walking with God, is a serious "labouring, that whether present or absent, we may be accepted of him." (2 Cor. v. 9.) To this the love of our Redeemer must constrain us: "For he died for all, that they which live, should not henceforth live unto themselves, but unto him that died for them, and rose again." (Ver. 14, 15.) Religion therefore is called the seeking of God, because the soul doth press after him, and labour to enjoy him, as the runner seeks to reach the prize; or as a suitor seeketh the love and fruition of the person beloved. And all the particular acts of religion are oft denominated from this intention of the end, and following after it, and are all called 'a seeking the Lord.' Conversion is called 'a seeking the Lord.' "Seek ye the Lord while he may be found." (Isa. lv. 6.) "The children of Israel shall return and seek the Lord their God." (Hos. iii. 5.) "They do not return to the Lord their God, nor seek him." (Hos. vii. 10.) Men that are called to conversion, are called to seek God. "Break up your fallow ground, for it is time to seek the Lord, till he come and rain righteousness upon you." (Hos. x. 12.) The converted children of "Israel and Judah shall go weeping together to seek the Lord their God." (Jer. l. 4.) The wicked are described to be men that "do not seek the Lord." (Isa. ix. 13; xxxi. 1.) The holy covenant was "to seek the Lord." (2 Chron. xv. 12, 13.) If therefore you would walk with God, let him be the mark, the prize, the treasure, the happiness, the heaven itself which you aim at, and sincerely seek. "Now set your heart and your soul to seek the Lord your God." (1 Chron. xxii. 19.) "Glory ye in his holy name. Let the heart of them rejoice that seek the Lord. Seek the Lord and his strength, seek his face for evermore." (Psal. cv. 3, 4.) As the life of a covetous man is a seeking of riches, and the life of an ambitious man is a seeking of worldly honour and applause, so the life of a man that liveth to God, is a seeking him; to please him, honour him, and enjoy him: and so much of this as he attaineth, so much doth he attain of satisfaction and content. If you live to God, and seek him as your end and all, the want of anything will be tolerable to you, which is but consistent with the fruition of his love. If he be pleased, man's displeasure may be borne. The loss of all things if Christ be won, will not undo us. Man's condemnation of us signifieth but little, if God the absolute Judge do justify us. He walketh not with God, that liveth not to him as his only happiness and end.

4. Moreover our walking with God includeth our subjection to his authority, and our taking his wisdom and will to be our guide, and his laws in nature and Scripture for our rule. You must not walk with him as his equals, but as his subjects: nor give him the honour of an ordinary superior, but of the universal King. In our doubts he must resolve us; and in our straits we must ask counsel of the Lord. "Lord, what wouldst thou have me to do," is one of the first words of a penitent soul. (Acts ix. 6.) When sensual worldlings do first ask the flesh, or those that can do it hurt or good, what they would have them be or do. None of Christ's true subjects, do call any man father or master on earth, but in subordination to their highest Lord. (Matt. xxiii.) The authority of God doth awe them, and govern them more than the fear of the greatest upon earth. Indeed they know no power but God's, and that which he committeth unto man. And therefore they can obey no man against God, whatever it cost them: but under God they are most readily and faithfully subject to their governors, not merely as to men that have power to hurt them if they disobey; but as to the officers of the Lord, whose authority they discern and reverence in them. But when they have to do with the enemies of Christ, who usurp a power which he never gave them against his kingdom and the souls of men, they think it easy to resolve the question, "Whether it be better to obey God or men?" As the commands of a rebellious constable, or other fellow-subject, are of no authority against the king's commands; so the commands of all the men on earth are of so small authority with them against the laws of God, that they fully approve of the ready and resolute answer of those witnesses, "We are not careful to answer thee in this matter. If it be so our God whom we serve is able to deliver us, &c. But if not, be it known unto thee, O king, that we will not serve thy gods, nor worship the golden image which thou hast set up." (Dan. iii. 16-18.) Worldlings are ruled by their fleshly interest, and wisdom, and self-will, and by the will of man so far as it doth comport with these. By these you may handle them and lead them up and down the world: by these doth Satan hold them in captivity. But believers feel themselves in subjection to a higher Lord, and better law, which they faithfully, though imperfectly observe. Therefore our walking with God is called a 'walking in his law;' (Exod. xvi. 4;) a 'walking in his statutes, and keeping and doing his commands;' (Lev. xxvi. 3;) 'walking in his paths.' (Mic. iv, 2.) It is our 'following the Lamb, which way soever he goeth:' To be given up to our own heart's lusts, and to walk in our counsels, is contrary to this holy walk with God, (Psal. lxxxi. 12.), and is the course of those that are departed from him: and they that are far from him shall perish: he destroyeth those that go a whoring

from him. But it is good for us to draw near to God. (Psal. lxxiii. 27, 28.)

5. Our walking with God doth imply that as we are ruled by his will, so we fear no punishment like his threatened displeasure: and that the threats of death from mortal men, will not prevail with us so much as his threats of hell. (Luke xii. 4.) If God say, 'I will condemn thee to everlasting punishment if thou wilt not keep my laws;' and if men say, 'We will condemn thee to imprisonment or death if thou keep them,' the believer more feareth God than man. The law of the king doth condemn Daniel to the lion's den, if he forbear not to pray for a certain time. But he more feareth God, that will deny those that deny him, and forsake those that forsake him. Therefore the forementioned witnesses ventured on the fiery furnace, because God threatened a more dreadful fire. Therefore a true believer dare not live, when an unbeliever dare not die: he dare not save his life from God, lest he lose it; but loseth it that he may save it. But unbelievers that walk not with God, but after the flesh, do most fear them that they observe most powerful in the world, and will more be moved with the penalty of some worldly loss or suffering, than with God's most dreadful threats of hell: for that which they see not, is to them as nothing, while they want that faith by which it is foreknown, and must be escaped.

6. Moreover he that walks with God, doth from God expect his full reward. He ceaseth not his holy course, though no man observe him, or none commend him or approve him; though all about him hate him and condemn him; though he be so far from gaining by it with men, that it cost him all that he hath or hoped for in the world: for he knoweth that godliness is of itself great gain, and that it "hath the promise of this life and that to come," and none can make God's promise void. He knoweth that his "Father which seeth in secret will reward him openly;" (Matt. vi.) and that he "shall have a treasure in heaven" that parteth with all on earth for Christ. (Luke xviii. 22.) And he hath such respect to this promised "recompence of reward," that for it he can "suffer with the people of God, and account the very reproach of Christ a greater treasure" than court or country can afford him in a way of sin. (Heb. xi. 26.) He accounteth them "blessed that are persecuted for righteousness sake, because the kingdom of heaven is theirs." He judgeth it a cause of exceeding joy, to be reviled, and, persecuted, and to have all manner of evil falsely spoken of us for the sake of Christ, because our reward in heaven is great. (Matt. v. 10-12.) For he verily believeth, that as sure as these transitory pleasures will have an end, and everlastingly forsake those miserable souls that were deluded by them, so certainly is there a life of endless joys, to be possessed in heaven with God and all the holy ones; and this he will trust to, as that which will fully repair his losses, and repay his cost, and not deceive him. Let others trust to what they will, it is this that he is resolved to trust to, and venture all to make it sure (when he is sure that all is nothing which he ventureth, and that by the adventure he can never be a loser, nor ever save by choosing that which itself must perish). Thus he that truly walks with God expecteth his reward from God, and with God, and thence is encouraged in all his duty, and thence is emboldened in all his conflicts, and thence is upheld and comforted in his sufferings. When man is the rewarder (as well as the chief ruler) of the hypocrite, and earthly things are the poise and motives to his earthly mind.

7. Our walking with God importeth that as we expect our reward from him, so also that we take his promise for our security for that reward. Believing his word and trusting his fidelity to the quieting and emboldening of the soul, is part of our holy walking with him. A promise of God is greater satisfaction and en-

couragement to a true believer, than all the visible things on earth. A promise of God can do more, and prevail further with an upright soul, than all the sensible objects in the world. He will do more, and go further upon such a promise, than he will for all that man can give him. Peruse the life of Christ's apostles, and see what a promise of Christ can do. How it made them forsake all earthly plea-sures, possessions and hopes, and part with friends, and houses, and country, and travel up and down the world, in dangers and sufferings, and unwearied labours, despised and abused by great and small: and all this to preach the Gospel of the kingdom, which they had never seen, and to attain that everlasting happiness, and help others to attain it, for which they had nothing but the promise of their Lord. See what a promise well believed will make a Christian do and suffer. Believers did those noble acts, and the martyrs underwent those torments, which are men-tioned Heb. xi. because "they judged him faithful that had promised." (Heb. xi. 11.) They considered not difficulties, and defect of means, and improbabilities as to second causes, nor "staggered at the promise of God through unbelief; but being strong in faith, gave glory to God; being fully persuaded, that what he had promised he was also able to perform." As it is said of Abraham, Rom. iv. 19-21.

8. To walk with God, is to live as in his presence, and that with desire and delight. When we believe and apprehend that wherever we are, we are before the Lord, who seeth our hearts and all our ways; who knoweth every thought we think, and every word we speak, and every secret thing which we do: as verily to believe that God is here present and observeth all, as we do that we ourselves are here. To compose our minds, our thoughts, our affections to that holy reverence and seriousness as beseemeth man before his Maker. To order our words with that care and gravity as beseems those that speak in the hearing of the Lord. That no man's presence do seem more considerable to us than his presence: as we are not moved at the presence of a fly, or worm, or dog, when persons of honour and reverence are present, so should we not comparatively be moved at the presence of man, how great, or rich, or terrible soever, when we know that God himself is present, to whom the greatest of the sons of men, are more inconsiderable than a fly or worm is unto them. As the presence of the king makes ordinary standers by to be unobserved, and the discourses of the learned make us disregard the bab-blings of children; so the presence of God should make the greatest to be scarce observed or regarded in comparison of him. God, who is still with us, should so much take up our regard, that all others in his presence should be but as a candle in the presence of the sun. Therefore it is that a believer composeth himself to that behaviour which he knoweth God doth most expect, and beseemeth those that stand before him. When others accommodate themselves to the persons that are present, observing them, pleasing them, and showing them respect, while they take no notice of God at all, as if they believed not that he is there. Hence it is that the men of God were wont to speak (though reverently, yet) familiarly of God, as children of their father with whom they dwell, as being indeed fellow-citizens with the saints, who are his household. Abraham calleth him, "The Lord before whom I walk." (Gen. xxiv. 40.) And Jacob, "God before whom my fathers Abra-ham and Isaac walked." (Gen. xlviii. 15.) And David resolveth, "I will walk be-fore the Lord in the land of the living." (Psal. cxvi. 9.) Yea God himself is pleased to use the terms of gracious, condescending familiarity with them. "Christ dwel-leth in them by faith." (Ephes. iii. 17.) His Spirit dwelleth in them as his house and temple. (Rom. viii. 9.) Yea the Father himself is said to dwell in them, and they in him, "He that keepeth his commandments dwelleth in him, and he in him." (1

John iii. 24.) "If we love one another, God dwelleth in us. Hereby we know that we dwell in him, and he in us, because he hath given us of his Spirit. Whoever shall confess that Jesus is the Son of God, God dwelleth in him, and he in God. God is love, and he that dwelleth in love, dwelleth in God, and God in him." (1 John iv. 12, 13, 15, 16.) Yea, God is said to walk in them, as they are said to walk with him; "For ye are the temple of the living God; as God hath said, I will dwell in them, and walk in them, and I will be their God, and they shall be my people." (2 Cor. vi. 16.)

Our walking with God then is not only a sense of that common presence which he must needs afford to all; but it is also a believing apprehension of his gracious presence, as our God and reconciled Father, with whom we dwell, being brought near unto him by Christ; and who dwelleth in us by his Spirit.

9. To walk with God (as here we are in flesh) includeth not only our believing his presence, but also that we see him (as the chief cause in the effects) in his creatures, and his daily providence, that we look not on creatures as independent or separated from God; but see them as the glass, and God as the represented face; and see them as the letters and words, and God as the sense of all the creatures that are the first book which he appointed man to read. We must behold his glory declared by the heavens, (Psal. xix. 1), and see him shining in the sun; and see his power in the fabric of the world, and his wisdom in the admirable order of the whole. We must taste the sweetness of his love in the sweetness of our food, and in the comforts of our friends, and all our accommodations; we must see, and love his image in his holy ones; and we must hear his voice in the ministry of his messengers. Thus every creature must become a preacher to us, and we must see the name of God upon it. And thus all things will be sanctified to us, while "Holiness to the Lord" is written upon all. Though we must not therefore make idols of the creatures, because God appeareth to us in them, yet must we hear the message which they bring us, and reverence in them the name of the Creator which they bear. By this way of conversing with them, they will not ensnare us, or deceive, or poison us, as they do the carnal, unbelieving world. But as the fish brought money to Peter to pay his tribute, so every creature would bring us a greater, even a spiritual gain. When we behold it, we should say with pleasant admiration, "This is the work of God, and it is wonderful in our eyes." This is the true divine philosophy, which seeketh, and findeth, and contemplateth, and admireth the great Creator in his works. When that which sticketh in the creature itself (whatever discovery it seem to make) is but a childish, unprofitable trifling: like learning to shape all the letters aright, without learning to know their signification and sense. It is God appearing in the creatures, this is the life, and beauty, and use, and excellency of all the creatures; without him they are but carcases, deformed, useless, vain, insignificant and very nothings.

10. Our walking with God, doth contain our willing and sincere attendance on him in the use of those holy duties in which he hath appointed us to expect his grace. He is everywhere in his essential presence, but he is not everywhere alike to be found in the communications of grace. The assemblies of his saints that worship him in holy communion, are places where he is more likely to be found than in an alehouse or a playhouse. You are more likely to have holy converse with him among the holy, that will speak of holy things to your edification, than among the senseless, ignorant sensualists, and the scornful enemies of holiness, that are the servants of the devil, whom he useth in his daily work for the deceiving and perdition of the world. Therefore the conversation of the wicked doth grieve and

vex the righteous soul, (as it is said the Sodomites did by Lot, 2 Peter ii. 7, 8), because all their conversation is ungodly, far from God, not savouring of any true knowledge of him, or love to him, but is against him by enmity and provocation. If God himself do dwell and walk in all his holy ones, then they that dwell and walk with them, have the best opportunity to dwell and walk with God. To converse with those in whom God dwelleth, is to converse with him in his image, and to attend him at his dwelling. And willfully to run among the wicked, is to run far away from God. "In his temple doth every man speak of his glory;" (Psal. xxix. 9), when among his brutish enemies every man speaketh to the dishonour of him in his word and ways. He is otherwise present with those that are congregated in his name and for his worship, than he is with those that are assembled for wickedness or vanity, or live as brutes without God in the world. And we must draw as near him as we can, if we would be such as walk with God.

We must not be strange to him in our thoughts, but make him the object of our most serious meditations. It is said of the wicked that "they are far from God;" and that "God is not in all their thoughts." (Psal. lxxiii. 27; x. 4) The thoughts are the mind's employment. It dwells on that which it frequently thinks of. It is a walk of the mind, and not of the body which we are treating of. To mind the world, and fleshly things, is contrary to this walk with God: we are far from him, when our thoughts are (ordinarily) far from him. I know that it is lawful and meet to think of the business of our callings, so far as is necessary to the prudent successful management of them: and that it is not requisite that our thoughts be always actually upon God: but he that doth manage his calling in holiness, doth all in obedience to God's commands, and sees that his work be the work of God, and he intendeth all to the glory of God, or the pleasing of his blessed will. And he oft reneweth these actual intentions; and oft interposeth thoughts of the presence, or power, or love, or interest of him whom he is serving: he often lifteth up his soul in some holy desire or ejaculatory request to God: he oft taketh occasion from what he seeth, or heareth, or is doing, for some more spiritual meditation or discourse: so that still it is God that his mind is principally employed on or for, even in his ordinary work (while he liveth as a Christian).

And it is not enough to think of God; but we must think of him as God; with such respect, and reverence, and love, and trust, and submission (in our measure) as is due from the creature to his Creator. For as some kind of speaking of him is but a taking his name in vain; so some kind of thinking of him is but a dishonouring of him, by contemptuous, or false, unworthy thoughts. Most of our walking with God consisteth in such affectionate apprehensions of him as are suitable to his blessed attributes and relations. All the day long our thoughts should be working either on God, or for God: either upon some work of obedience which he hath imposed on us, and in which we desire to please and honour him, or else directly upon himself. Our hearts must be taken up in contemplating and admiring him, in magnifying his name, his word and works; and in pleasant contentful thoughts of his benignity, and of his glory, and the glory which he conferreth on his saints. He that is unskillful or unable to manage his own thoughts with some activity, seriousness and order, will be a stranger to much of the holy converse which believers have with God. They that have given up the government of their thoughts, and turned them loose to go which way fantasy pleaseth, and present sensitive objects do invite them, and to run up and down the world as masterless, unruly vagrants, can hardly expect to keep them in any constant attendance upon God, or readiness for any sacred work. And the sudden thoughts which they have of God, will be rude and stupid, savouring more of profane contempt, than of holiness, when they should be reverent, serious, affectionate and practical, and such as conduce to a holy composure of their hearts and lives.

And as we must walk with God, 1. In our communion with his servants; 2. And in our affectionate meditations; so also, 3. In all the ordinances which he hath appointed for our edification and his worship.

1. The reading of the word of God, and the explication and application of it in good books, is a means to possess the mind with sound, and orderly, and working apprehensions of God, and of his holy truths: so that in such reading our understandings are oft illustrated with a heavenly light, and our hearts are touched with a special delightful relish of that truth, and they are secretly attracted and engaged unto God, and all the powers of our souls are excited and animated to a holy, obedient life.

2. The same word preached with a lively voice, with clearness and affection, hath a greater advantage for the same illumination and excitation of the soul. When a minister of Christ that is truly a divine, being filled with the knowledge and love of God, shall copiously and affectionately open to his hearers, the excellencies which he hath seen, and the happiness which he hath foreseen and tasted of himself, it frequently (through the co-operation.of the Spirit of Christ) doth wrap up the hearers' hearts to God, and bring them into a more lively knowledge of him, actuating their graces, and inflaming their hearts with a heavenly love, and such desires as God hath promised to satisfy. Christ doth not only send his ministers furnished with authority from him, but also furnished with his Spirit, to speak of spiritual things in a spiritual manner; so that in both respects he might say, "He that heareth you, heareth me:" and also by the same Spirit doth open and excite the hearts of the hearers. So that it is God himself that a serious Christian is principally employed with, in the hearing of his heavenly, transforming word: and therefore he is affected with reverence and holy fear, with some taste of heavenly delight, with obediential subjection and resignation of himself to God. The word of God is powerful, not only in pulling down all high exalting thoughts, that rise up against God, but also in lifting up depressed souls, that are unable to rise unto heavenly knowledge, or communion with God. If some Christians could but always find as much of God upon their hearts at other times, as they find sometimes under a spiritual, powerful ministry, they would not so complain that they seem forsaken, and strangers to all communion with God, as many of them do. While God (by his messengers and Spirit) is speaking, and man is hearing him; while God is treating with man about his reconciliation and everlasting happiness, and man is seriously attending to the treaty and motions of his Lord, surely this is a very considerable part of our walking and converse with God.

3. Also in the sacrament of the body and blood of Christ, we are called to a familiar converse with God. He there appeareth to us by a wonderful condescension in the representing, communicating signs of the flesh and blood of his Son, in which he hath most conspicuously revealed his love and goodness to believers: there Christ himself with his covenant-gifts are all delivered to us by these investing signs of his own institution; even as knighthood is given by a sword, and as a house is delivered by a key, or land by a twig and turf. Nowhere is God so near to man as in Jesus Christ: and nowhere is Christ so familiarly represented to us, as in this holy sacrament. Here we are called to sit with him at his table, as his invited welcome guests; to commemorate his sacrifice, to feed upon his very flesh and blood; that is, with our mouths upon his representative flesh and blood,

and with our applying faith upon his real flesh and blood, by such a feeding as belongs to faith. The marriage-covenant betwixt God incarnate, and his espoused ones, is there publicly sealed, celebrated and solemnized. There we are entertained by God as friends, and not as servants only, and that at the most precious costly feast. If ever a believer may on earth expect his kindest entertainment, and near access, and a humble intimacy with his Lord, it is in the participation of his sacrifice-feast, which is called 'The Communion,' because it is appointed as well for our special communion with Christ as with one another. It is here that we have the fullest intimation, expression and communication of the wondrous love of God; and therefore it is here that we have the loudest call, and best assistance, to make a large return of love: and where there is most of this love between God and man, there is most communion, and most of heaven, that can be had on earth.

But it much concerneth the members of Christ, that they deprive not themselves of this communion with God in this holy sacrament through their miscarriage; which is too frequently done by one of these extremes. Either by rushing upon holy things with a presumptuous, careless, common frame of heart, as if they knew not that they go to feast with Christ, and discerned not his body: or else by an excess of fear, drawing back and questioning the goodwill of God, and thinking diminutively of his love and mercy. By this means Satan depriveth many of the comfortable part of their communion with God, both in this sacrament, and in other ways of grace: and maketh them avoid him as an enemy, and be loath to come into his special presence; and even to be afraid to think of him, to pray to him, or to have any holy converse with him: when the just belief and observation of his love would establish them, and revive their souls with joy, and give them experience of the sweet delights which are opened to them in the Gospel, and which believers find in the love of God, and the foretaste of the everlasting pleasures.

4. In holy, faithful, fervent prayer, a Christian hath very much of his converse with God. For prayer is our approach to God, and calling to mind his presence and his attributes, and exercising all his graces in a holy motion towards him, and an exciting all the powers of our souls to seek him, attend him and reverently to worship him. It is our treating with him about the most important businesses in all the world: a begging of the greatest mercies, and a deprecating his most grievous judgments; and all this with the nearest familiarity that man in flesh can have with God. In prayer, the Spirit of God is working up our hearts unto him, with desires expressed in sighs and groans: it is a work of God as well as of man: he bloweth the fire, though it be our hearts that burn and boil. In prayer we lay hold on Jesus Christ, and plead his merits and intercession with the Father: he taketh us as it were by the hand, and leadeth us unto God, and hideth our sins, and procureth our acceptance, and presenteth us amiable to his Father, having justified and sanctified us, and cleansed us from those pollutions, which rendered us loathsome; and abominable. To speak to God in serious prayer, is a work so high, and of so great moment, that it calleth off our minds from all things else, and giveth no creature room or leave to look into the soul, or once to be observed; The mind is so taken up with God, and employed with him, that creatures are forgotten, and we take no notice of them (unless when through the diversions of the flesh, our prayers are interrupted and corrupted, and so far degenerate, and are no prayer; so far I say as we thus turn away from God). So that the soul that is most and best at prayer, is most and best at walking with God, and hath most communion with him in the Spirit. And to withdraw from prayer, is to withdraw from God. And to be unwill-

ing to pray, is to be unwilling to draw near to God. Meditation or contemplation is a duty in which God is much enjoyed. But prayer hath meditation in it, and much more. All that is upon the mind in meditation, is upon the mind in prayer, and that with great advantage, as being presented before God, and pleaded with him, and so animated by the apprehensions of his observing presence, and actuated by the desires and pleadings of the soul. When we are commanded to pray, it includeth a command to repent, and believe, and fear the Lord, and desire his grace. For faith and repentance, and fear and desire, are altogether in action in a serious prayer; and, as it were, naturally each one takes his place, and there is a holy order in the acting of these graces in a Christian's prayers, and a harmony which he doth seldom himself observe. He that in meditation knoweth not how to be regular and methodical, when he is studiously contriving and endeavouring it, yet in prayer before he is aware, hath repentance, and faith, and fear, and desire, and every grace fall in its proper place and order, and contribute its part to the performance of the work. The new nature of a Christian is more immediately and vigorously operative in prayer, than in many other duties: and therefore every infant in the family of God can pray (with groaning desires, and ordered graces, if not with well-ordered words). When Paul began to live to Christ, he began (aright) to pray: "Behold he prayeth," saith God to Ananias. (Acts ix. 11.) And "because they are sons, God sends the Spirit of his Son into the hearts of his elect, even the Spirit of Adoption, by which they cry Abba, Father," (Gal. iv. 6.), as children naturally cry to their parents for relief. And nature is more regular in its works than art or human contrivance is. Necessity reacheth many a beggar to pray better for relief to men, than many learned men (that feel not their necessities) can pray to God. The Spirit of God is a better methodist than we are. And though I know that we are bound to use our utmost care and skill for the orderly actuating of each holy affection in our prayers, and not pretend the sufficiency of the Spirit for the patronage of our negligence or sloth (for the Spirit makes use of our understandings for the actuating of our wills and affections); yet withal it cannot be denied, but that it was upon a special reason that the Spirit that is promised to believers is called a "spirit of grace and supplication." (Zech. xii. 10.) And that it is given us to "help our infirmities," even the infirmities of our understanding, when "we know not what to pray for as we ought." (Rom. viii. 26.) And that the Spirit itself is said to "make intercession for us, with groanings which cannot be uttered." It is not the Spirit without, that is here meant: such intercession is nowhere ascribed to that. How then is the prayer of the Spirit within us distingushed from our prayer? Not as different effects of different causes: as different prayers by these different parties. But as the same prayer proceeding from different causes, having a special force (for quality and degree) as from one cause (the Spirit), which it hath not from the other cause (from ourselves), except as received from the Spirit. The Spirit is a new nature or fixed inclination in the saints: for their very self-love and will to good, is sanctified in them, which works so readily (though voluntarily) as that it is in a sort by the way of nature, though not excluding reason and will; and not as the motion of the brutish appetite. And that God is their felicity, and the only help and comfort of their souls, and so the principal good to be desired by them, is become to them a truth so certain, and beyond all doubt, that their understandings are convinced that 'velle bonum,' and 'velle Deum,' to love good, and to love God, are words that have almost the same signification; and therefore here is no room for deliberation and choice, where there is 'omnimoda ratio boni,' nothing but unquestionable good. A Christian (so far as he is such) cannot choose but desire the favour and fruition of God in immortality, even as he cannot choose (because he is a man) but desire his own felicity in general. And as he cannot (as a man) but be unwilling of destruction, and cannot but fear apparent misery, and that which bringeth it; so as a Christian he cannot choose but be unwilling of damnation, and of the wrath of God, and of sin as sin, and fear the apparent danger of his soul, so that his new nature will presently cast his fear, and repentance, and desires into their proper course and order, and set them on work on their several objects (about the main unquestionable things, however they may err, or need more deliberation about things doubtful). The new creature is not as a lifeless engine (as a clock, or watch, or ship), where every part must be set in order by the art and hand of man, and so kept and used. But it is more like the frame of our own nature, even like man who is a living engine, when every part is set in its place and order by the Creator, and hath in itself a living and harmonical principle, which disposeth it to action, and to regular action, and is so to be kept in order and daily exercise by ourselves, as yet to be principally ordered and actuated, by the Spirit which is the principal cause.

By all which you may understand how the Holy Ghost is in us a Spirit of supplication, and helpeth our infirmities, and teacheth us to pray, and intercedeth in us; and also that prayer is to the new man so natural a motion of the soul towards God, that much of our walking with God is exercised in this holy duty: and that it is to the new life as breathing to our natural life; and therefore no wonder that we are commanded to "pray continually," (1 Thess. v. 17), as we must breathe continually, or as nature which needeth a daily supply of food for nourishment, hath a daily appetite to the food which it needeth, so hath the spiritual nature to its necessary food, and nothing but sickness doth take it off.

And thus I have showed how our walking with God, containeth a holy use of his appointed means.

11. To walk with God includeth our dependance on him for our receivings, and taking our mercies as from his hand. To live as upon his love and bounty; as children with their father, that can look for nothing but from him. As the eye of a servant, yea, of a craving dog, is upon his master's face and hand, so must our eye be on the Lord, for the gracious supply of all our wants. If men give us anything, we take them but as the messengers of God, by whom he sendeth it us. We will not be unthankful to men; but we thank them but for bringing us our Father's gifts. Indeed man is so much more than a mere messenger, as that his own charity also is exercised in the gift. A mere messenger is to do no more but obediently to deliver what is sent us, and he need not exercise any charity of his own; and we owe him thanks only for his fidelity and labour, but only to his master for the gift. But God will so far honour man, as that he shall be called also to use his charity, and distribute his master's gifts with some self-denial; and we owe him thanks, as under God, he partaketh in the charity of the gift; and as one child oweth thanks to another, who both in obedience to the father, and love to his brother, doth give some part of that which his father had given him before. But still it is from our Father's bounty, as the principal cause that all proceeds. Thus Jacob speaketh of God, "God, before whom my fathers, Abraham and Isaac did walk, the God which fed me all my life long unto this day, the angel which redeemed me from all evil, bless the lads," &c. (Gen. xlviii. 15, 16.) When he had mentioned his father Abraham and Isaac's walking with God, he describeth his own by his dependence upon God, and receiving from him, acknowledging him the God that had fed him, and

delivered him all his life. Carnal men that live by sense, do depend upon inferior sensible causes; and though they are taught to pray to God, and thank him with their tongues, it is indeed their own contrivances and industry, or their visible benefactors, which their hearts depend upon and thank. It were a shame to them to be so plain as Pharaoh, and to say, "Who is the Lord?" or to speak as openly as Nebuchadnezzar, and say, "Is not this great Babylon that I have built, by the might of my power," &c. (Dan. iv. 30.) Yet the same atheism and self-idolizing is in their hearts, though it be more modestly and cunningly expressed. Hence it is that they that walk with God, have all their receivings sanctified to them, and have in all a divine and spiritual sweetness, which those that take them but as from creatures, do never feel or understand.

12. Lastly, It is contained in our walking with God, that the greatest business of our lives be with him, and for him. It is not a walk for compliment or recreation only, that is here meant; but it is a life of nearness, converse, and employment, as a servant or child that dwelleth with his master or father in the house. God should be always so regarded, that man should stand by as nothing, and be scarce observed in comparison of him. We should begin the day with God, and entertain him in the first and sweetest of our thoughts. We should walk abroad and do our works as in his sight. We must resolve to do no work but his, no not in our trades and ordinary callings. We must be able to say, It is the work which my Master set me to do, and I do it to obey and please his will. At night we must take an account of ourselves, and spread open that account before him, desiring his acceptance of what was well, and his pardon for what we did amiss, that we may thus be ready for our last account. In a word, though men be our fellow-labourers and companions, yet the principal business of our care and diligence, must be our Master's service in the world. And therefore we must look about us, and discern the opportunities of serving him, and of the best improvement of his talents; and must make it our daily study and business, to do him the greatest service we are able, whatever it may cost us through the malice of the enemies, being sure our labour shall not be in vain, and that we cannot serve him at too dear a rate. It is not as idle companions, but as servants, as soldiers, as those that put forth all their strength, to do his work and reach the crown, that we are called to walk with God. And all this is done, though not in the same degree by all, yet according to the measure of their holiness by every one that lives by faith.

Having told you what it is to walk with God, as to the matter of it, I shall more briefly tell you as to the manner. The nature of God, of man, and of the work, will tell it you.

1. That our walk with God must be with the greatest reverence: were we ever so much assured of his special love to us, and never so full of faith and joy, our reverence must be never the less for this. Though love cast out that guilty fear which discourageth the sinner from hoping and seeking for the mercy which would save him, and which disposeth him to hate and fly from God, yet doth it not cast out that reverence of God, which we owe him as his creatures, so infinitely below him as we are. It cannot be that God should be known and remembered as God, without some admiring and awful apprehensions of him. Infiniteness, omnipotency, and inaccessible majesty and glory, must needs affect the soul that knoweth them, with reverence and self-abasement. Though "we receive a kingdom that cannot be moved," yet if we will "serve God acceptably," we must "serve him with reverence and godly fear," as knowing he "is our God," so he is

also a "consuming fire." (Heb. xii. 28, 29.) We must so worship him as those that remember that we are worms and guilty sinners, and that he is most high and holy, and will be "sanctified in them that come nigh him, and before all the people he will be glorified." (Lev. x. 3.) Unreverence showeth a kind of atheistical contempt of God, or else a sleepiness and inconsiderateness of the soul. The sense of the goodness and love of God, must consist with the sense of his holiness and omnipotency. It is presumption, pride, or blockish stupidity, which excludeth reverence; which faith doth cause, and not oppose.

2. Our walking with God must be a work of humble boldness and familiarity. The reverence of his holiness and greatness, must not overcome or, exclude the sense of his goodness and compassion, nor the full assurance of faith and hope. Though by sin we are enemies and strangers to God, and stand afar off, yet in Christ we are reconciled to him, and brought near. (Ephes. ii. 13.) "For he is our peace, who hath taken down the partition, and abolished the enmity, and reconciled Jew and Gentile unto God." (ver. 14-16.) "And through him we have all an access to the Father by one Spirit. We are now no more strangers and foreigners, but fellow-citizens of the saints, and of the household of God." (ver. 18, 19.) "In him we have boldness and access with confidence by the belief of him." (Ephes. iii. 12.) Though of ourselves we are unworthy to be called his children, and may well stand afar off with the publican, and not dare to lift up our faces towards heaven, but smite our breasts, and say, "O Lord be merciful to me a sinner." Yet "have we boldness to enter into the holiest, by the blood of Jesus, by a new and living way which he hath consecrated for us, through the veil, that is to say, his flesh. And having an High Priest over the house of God, we may draw near with a true heart in full assurance of faith." (Heb. x. 19-22.) Therefore whensoever we are afraid at the sight of sin and justice, let us remember that "we have a great High Priest that is passed into the heavens, even Jesus the Son of God. And therefore let us come boldly to the throne of grace, that we may obtain mercy, and find grace to help in time of need." (Heb. iv. 14-16.) He that alloweth us to walk with him, doth allow us such humble familiarity as beseemeth those that walk together with him.

3. Our walking with God must be a work of some holy pleasure and delight. We may willingly be dragged into the presence of an enemy, and serve as drudges upon mere necessity or fear. But walking together is the loving and delightful converse of friends. When we take sweet counsel of the Lord, and set him always at our right hand, and are glad to hear from him, and glad to speak to him, and glad to withdraw our thoughts from all the things and persons in the world, that we may solace ourselves in the contemplations of his excellency, and the admirations of his love and glory, this is indeed to walk with God. You converse with him as with a stranger, an enemy, or your destroyer, and not as with God, while you had rather be far from him, and only tremble in his presence, and are glad when you have done and are got away, but have no delight or pleasure in him. If we can take delight in our walking with a friend, a friend that is truly loving and constant, a friend that is learned, wise and holy! if their wise and heavenly discourse be better to us, than our recreations, meat, or drink, or clothes! What delight then should we find in our secret converse with the most high, most wise and gracious God! How glad should we be to find him willing and ready to entertain us! How glad should we be that we may employ our thoughts on so high and excellent an object! What cause have we to say, "My meditation of him shall be sweet, and I will

be glad in the Lord." (Psal. civ. 34.) "In the multitude of my thoughts within me (my sorrowful, troublesome, weary thoughts) thy comforts do delight my soul." (Psal. xciv. 19.) Let others take pleasure in childish vanity or sensuality, but say thou as David, "I have rejoiced in the ways of thy commandments, as much as in all riches. I will meditate in thy precepts, and have respect unto thy ways. I will delight myself in thy statutes, and will not forget thy word. I will delight myself in thy commandments which I have loved." (Psal. cxix. 14-16, 47.) Let "scorners delight in scorning, and fools hate knowledge," (Prov. i. 22.), but "make me to go in the path of thy commandments, for therein do I delight." (Psal. cxix. 35.) If thou wouldst experimentally know the safety and glory of a holy life, "delight thyself in the Lord, and he shall give thee the desire of thy heart." (Psal. xxxvii. 4.) Especially when we draw near him in his solemn worship, and when we separate ourselves on his holy days from all our common worldly thoughts, to be conversant, as in heaven, with the blessed God; then may we with the holy apostle be "in the Spirit on the Lord's day," (Rev. i. 10.), "and if we turn away our foot from the Sabbath, from doing our pleasure on that holy day, and call the Sabbath a delight, the holy of the Lord, honourable, and shall honour him, not doing our own ways, nor finding our own pleasure, nor speaking our own words, then shall we delight ourselves in the Lord," (Isa. lviii. 13, 14.), and understand how great a privilege it is, to have the liberty of those holy days and duties for our sweet and heavenly converse with God.

4. Our walking with God must be a matter of industry and diligence. It is not an occasional idle converse, but a life of observance, obedience, and employment, that this phrase importeth. The sluggish, idle wishes of the hypocrite, whose hands refuse to labour, are not this walking with God: nor "the sacrifice of fools," who are hasty to utter the overflowings of their fantasy before the Lord, while they "keep not their foot, nor hearken to the law, nor consider that they do evil." (Eccles. v. 1-3.) "He that cometh to God (and will walk with him) must believe that he is, and that he is the rewarder of them that diligently seek him. God is with you, while you are with him; but if you forsake him, he will forsake you." (2 Chron. xv. 2.) "Up and be doing, and the Lord will be with you." (1 Chron. xxii. 16.) If you would meet with God in the way of mercy "take diligent heed to do the commandment and law, to love the Lord your God, and to walk in all his ways, and to cleave unto him, and to serve him with all your heart, and with all your soul." (Josh. xxii. 5.)

5. Our walking with God is a matter of some constancy. It signifieth our course and trade of life, and not some accidental action on the by. A man may walk with a stranger for a visit, or in compliment, or upon some unusual occasion. But this walk with God, is the act of those that dwell with him in his family, and do his work. It is not only to step and speak with him, or cry to him for mercy in some great extremity, or to go to church for company or custom, or think or talk of him sometimes heartlessly on the by, as a man will talk of news, or matters that are done in a foreign land, or of persons that we have little to do with. But it is to "be always with him." (Luke xv. 31.) "To seek first his kingdom and righteousness." (Matt. vi. 33.) "Not to labour (comparatively) for the food that perisheth, but for that which endureth to everlasting life." (John vi. 27.) "To delight in the law of the Lord, and meditate in it day and night." (Psal. i. 2.) That his "words be in our hearts, and that we teach them diligently to our children, and talk of them

sitting in the house, and walking by the way, lying down, and rising up," &c. (Deut. vi. 6, 8.) That "we pray continually." (1 Thess. v. 17.) "And in all things give thanks." But will the hypocrite delight himself in the Almighty, or will he always call upon God?" (Job xxvii. 10.) "His goodness is as the morning cloud, and as the early dew it goeth away." (Hos. vi. 4.)

So much of the description of this 'walking with God.'

Chapter II.

Use. We are next to consider how far this doctrine doth concern ourselves, and what use we have to make of it upon our hearts and lives.

And First, It acquainteth us with the abundance of atheism that is in the world, even among those that profess the knowledge of God. It is atheism not only to say, "There is no God;" but to say so "in the heart." (Psal. xiv. 1.) While the heart is no more affected towards him, observant of him, or confident in him, or submissive to him, than if indeed there were no God. When there is nothing of God upon the heart, no love, no fear, no trust, no subjection, this is heart atheism. When men that have some kind of knowledge of God, yet glorify him not "as God, nor are thankful to him, but become vain in their imaginations, and their foolish hearts are darkened; these men are heart-atheists; and professing themselves wise, they become fools, and are given up to vile affections. And as they do not like to retain God in their knowledge (however they may discourse of him, so) God oft giveth them over to a reprobate mind, to do those things that are not convenient, being filled with all unrighteousness, fornication, wickedness, covetousness, maliciousness, envy, murder, debate, deceit, malignity," &c. (Rom. i. 21,22, 26, 28-30.) Swarms of such atheists go up and down under the self-deceiving name of Christians. Being indeed unbelieving and defiled, so void of purity, that they deride it, and "nothing is pure to them; but even their mind and conscience is defiled. They profess that they know God, but they deny him in their works, being abominable and disobedient, and to every good work reprobate." (Titus i. 15, 16.) What are they but atheists, when "God is not in all their thoughts," (Psal. x. 4.), unless it be in their impious or blaspheming thoughts, or in their slight contemptuous thoughts! To take God for God indeed, and for our God, essentially includeth the taking him to be the most powerful, wise and good, the most just and holy, the Creator, Preserver and Governor of the world, whom we and all men are obliged absolutely to obey and fear, to love and desire, whose will is our beginning, rule and end. He that taketh not God for such as here described, taketh him not for God, and therefore is indeed an atheist. What name soever he assumeth to himself, this is the name that God will call him by; even a "fool that hath said in his heart there is no God: while they are corrupt and do abominably, they understand not, and seek not after God; they are all gone aside, and are altogether become filthy, there is none of them that doth good; they are workers of iniquity, they have no knowledge, and eat up the people of God as bread, and call not upon the Lord." (Psal. xiv. 1-4.) Ungodliness is but the English for atheism. The atheist or ungodly in opinion, is he that thinks that there is no God, or that he is one that we need not love and serve (and that is but the same, *viz.* to be no God). The atheist or ungodly in heart, or will, is he that consenteth not that God shall be his God, to be loved, feared, and obeyed before all. The atheist in life, or outward practice, is he that liveth as without God in the world; that seeketh him not as his chiefest good, and obeyeth him not as his highest absolute Lord; so that indeed atheism is the sum of all iniquity,

as godliness is the sum of all religion and moral good. If you see by the description which I have given you, what it is to be godly, and to walk with God, and
what it is to be an atheist or ungodly, you may easily see that godliness is more
rare, and atheism more common, than many that themselves are atheists will believe. It is not that which a man calls his God, that is taken by him for his God
indeed. It is not the tongue, but the heart that is the man. Pilate called Christ the
King of the Jews, when he crucified him. The Jews called God their Father, when
Christ telleth them, they were of their father the devil, and proveth it because
(whatever they said) they would do their lusts. (John viii. 44.) The same Jews
pretended to honour the name of the Messiah, and expect him, while they killed
him. The question is not what men call themselves, but what they are. Not whether you say you take God for your God, but whether you do so indeed. Not whether
you profess yourselves to be atheists, but whether you are atheists indeed or not.
If you are not, look over what I have here said, and ask your consciences, Do you
walk with God? who is it you submit yourselves willingly to be disposed of by?
to whom are you most subject? and whose commands have the most effectual
authority with you? who is the chief Governor of your hearts and lives? whom is
it that you principally desire to please? whom do you most fear? and whose displeasure do you principally avoid? from whom is it that you expect your greatest
reward? and in whom, and with whom do you place and expect your happiness?
whose work is it that you do, as the greatest business of your lives? Is it the goodness of God in himself, and unto you, that draweth up your hearts to him in love?
Is he the ultimate end of the main intentions, design, and industry of your lives?
Do you trust upon his word as your security for your everlasting hopes and happiness? Do you study and observe him in his works? Do you really live as in his
presence? Do you delight in his word, and meditate on it? Do you love the communion of saints and to be most frequent and familiar with them that are most
frequent and familiar with Christ? Do you favour more the particular affectionate
discourse about his nature, will and kingdom, than the frothy talk of empty wits,
or the common discourse of carnal worldlings? Do you love to be employed in
thanking him for his mercies, and in praising him, and declaring the glory of his
attributes and works? Is your dependence on him as your great Benefactor, and do
you receive your mercies as his gifts? If thus your principal observation be of
God, and your chief desire after God, and your chiefest confidence in God, and
your chiefest business in the world be with God, and for God, and your chiefest
joy be in the favour of God, (when you can apprehend it) and in the prosperity of
his church, and your hopes of glory; and your chiefest grief and trouble be your
sinful distance from him, and your backwardness and disability in his love and
service, and the fear of his displeasure, and the injuries done to his Gospel and
honour in the world; then I must needs say, you are savingly delivered from your
atheism and ungodliness; you do not only talk of God, but walk with God; you are
then acquainted with that spiritual life and work, which the sensual world is unacquainted with, and with those invisible, everlasting excellencies, which if worldlings knew, they would change their minds, and choice, and pleasures. You are
then acquainted with that rational, manly, saintlike life, which ungodly men are
strangers to; and you are in the way of that well-grounded hope and peace to
which all the pleasures and crowns on earth, if compared, are but cheats and misery. But if you were never yet brought to walk with God, do not think you have a
sound belief in God, nor that you acknowledge him sincerely, nor that you are
saved from heart-atheism: nor is it piety in the opinion and the tongue, that will

save him that is an atheist, or ungodly in heart and life. Divinity is an affective-practical science. Knowing is not the ultimate or perfective act of man: but a means to holy love, and joy, and service. Nor is it clear and solid knowledge, if it do not somewhat affect the heart, and engage and actuate the life, according to the nature and use of the thing known. The soundness of knowledge and belief, is not best discerned in the intellectual acts themselves, but in their powerful, free and pleasant efficacy, upon our choice and practice. By these therefore you must judge, whether you are godly or atheistical. The question is not what your tongues say of God, nor what complimental ceremonious observances you allow him, but what your hearts and your endeavours say of him, and whether you glorify him as God, when you say you know him: otherwise you will find that the "wrath of God is revealed from heaven, against all ungodliness and unrighteousness of men, who hold the truth in unrighteousness." (Rom. i. 18, 21.)

And now, alas! what matter of lamentation is here before us! To see how seriously men converse with one another; and how God is overlooked or neglected by the most! How men live together, as if there were more that is considerable and regardable in these particles of animated dust, than in the Lord Almighty, and in all his graces, service and rewards! To see how God is cast aside, and his interest made to give place to the interest of the flesh, and his services must stay till men have done their service to their lusts, or to worldly men, that can do them hurt, or show them favour! And his will must not be done, when it crosseth the will of sinful man! How little do all the commands, and promises, and threatenings of God signify, with these atheistical men, in comparison of their lusts, or the laws of men, or anything that concerneth their temporal prosperity! O how is the world revolted from their Maker! How have they lost the knowledge of themselves, and forgotten their natures, capacities and obligations, and what it is to be indeed a man! O hearken, sinners, to the call of your Redeemer! Return, O seduced, wandering souls, and know at last your resting place! Why is not God in all your thoughts? or why is he thought on with so much remissness, unwillingness, and contempt! and with so little pleasure, seriousness, or regard? Do you understand yourselves in this? Do you deal worthily with God? or wisely for yourselves? Do you take more pleasure, with the prodigal, to feed swine, and to feed with swine, than to dwell at home with your heavenly Father? and to walk before him, and serve him in the world? Did you but know how dangerous a way you have been in, and how unreasonably you have dealt, to forsake God in your hearts, and follow that which cannot profit you, what haste would you make to leave the crowd, and come home to God, and try a more noble and gainful conversation? If reasons may have room and leave to work upon you, I will set a few before you more distinctly, to call you off from your barren, inordinate creature-converse, to a believing, serious converse with God.

1. The higher and more excellent the object is (especially when it is also of most concernment to ourselves), the more excellent is the converse. Therefore as nothing dare compare itself with God, so no employment may be compared with this of holy walking with him. How vile a contempt is it of the Almighty, and of our celestial joys, for the heart to neglect them, and turn away, and dwell upon vanity and trouble, and let these highest pleasures go! Is not God and glory worthy of thy thoughts, and all thy service?

2. What are those things that take thee up? Are they better than God? or fitter to supply thy wants? If thou think, and trust in them accordingly, ere long thou shalt know better what they are, and have enough of thy cursed choice and confi-

dence. Tell those that stand by thee at the parting hour, whether thou didst choose aright and make a gaining or a saving match. O poor sinners! have you not yet warning enough to satisfy you that all things below are vanity and vexation, and that all your hope of happiness is above? Will not the testimony of God satisfy you? Will not the experience of the world for so many thousand years together satisfy you? Will not the ill success of the damned satisfy you? Will nothing but your own experience convince you? If so, consider well the experience you have already made, and seasonably retire, and try no further, and trust not so dangerous a deceiver to the last, lest you buy your knowledge at a dearer rate than you will now believe.

3. You have daily more to do with God, than with all the world, whether you will or no. And therefore seeing you cannot avoid him if you would, prefer that voluntary obediential converse, which hath a reward, before that necessitated converse which hath none. You are always in his hands: he made you for his service; and he will dispose of you and all that you have, according to his will. It shall not go with you as yourselves would have it, nor as your friends would have it, nor as princes and great ones of the world would have it; (unless as their wills comply with God's) but as God would have it, who will infallibly accomplish all his will. If a sparrow fall not to the ground without him, and all the hairs of our heads are numbered, then certainly he overruleth all your interests and affairs, and they are absolutely at his disposal. To whom then in reason should you so much apply yourselves as unto him? If you will not take notice of him, he will take notice of you: he will remember you, whether you remember him or not; but it may be with so strict and severe a remembrance, as may make you wish he did quite forget you. You are always in his presence; and can you then forget him, and hold no voluntary converse with him, when you stand before him? If it be but mean, inferior persons that we dwell with, and are still in company with, we mind them more, and speak more to them, than we do to greater persons that we seldom see. But in God there is both greatness and nearness to invite you. Should not all the worms on earth stand by, while the glorious God doth call you to him, and offer you the honour and happiness of his converse? Shall the Lord of heaven and earth stand by, and be shut out, while you are chatting or trifling with his creatures? Nay, shall he be neglected that is always with you? You cannot remove yourselves a moment from his sight; and therefore you should not shut your eyes, and turn away your face, and refuse to observe him who is still observing you.

Moreover, your dependence, both for soul and body, is all on him. You can have nothing desirable but by his gift. He feeds you, he clotheth you, he maintaineth you, he gives you life, and breath, and all things; and yet can you overlook him, or forget him? Do not all his mercies require your acknowledgment? A dog will follow him that feedeth him: his eye will be upon his master. And shall we live upon God, and yet forget and disregard him? We are taught a better use of his mercies by the holy prophet; "O bless our God, ye people, and make the voice of his praise to be heard: which holdeth our soul in life, and suffereth not our feet to be moved!" (Psal. lxvi. 8, 9.)

Nay, it is not yourselves alone, but all the world that depends on God. It is his power that supporteth them, and his will that disposeth of them, and his bounty that provideth for them: and therefore he must be the observation and admiration of the world. It is less unreasonable to take no notice of the earth that beareth us and yieldeth us fruit, and of the sun that yieldeth us heat and light, them to disregard the Lord that is more to us than sun, and earth, and all things. "The eyes of all things wait on him; and he giveth them their meat in season. He openeth his hand and satisfieth the desire of every living thing." (Psal. cxlv. 15, 16.) "The Lord is good to all, and his tender mercies are over all his works. All his works therefore shall praise him, and his saints shall bless him. They shall speak of the glory of his kingdom, and talk of his power." (ver. 10, 11.)

Moreover God is so abundantly and wonderfully represented to us in all his works, as will leave us under the guilt of most unexcusable contempt, if we overlook him, and live as without him in the world. "The heavens declare the glory of God, and the firmament showeth his handy work. Day unto day uttereth speech, and night unto night showeth knowledge." (Psal. xix. 1, 2.) Thus "that which may be known of God is manifest; for the invisible things of him from the creation of the world, are clearly seen, being understood by the things that are made, even his eternal power and Godhead; so that the ungodly are without excuse." (Rom. i. 19, 20.) Cannot you see that which all the world revealeth; nor hear that which all the world proclaimeth? "O sing ye forth the honour of his name: make his praise glorious! Say to the Lord, How terrible art thou in thy works! Through the greatness of thy power shall thine enemies submit themselves unto thee. All the earth shall worship thee, and shall sing unto thee: they shall sing unto thy name: come and see the works of God: he is terrible in his doings towards the children of men." (Psal. lxvi. 2-5.) Can we pass him by, that is everywhere present, and by every creature represented to us? Can we forget him, when all the world are our remembrancers? Can we stop our ears against the voice of heaven and earth? Can we be ignorant of him, when the whole creation is our teacher? Can we overlook that holy, glorious name, which is written so legibly upon all things that ever our eyes beheld, that nothing but blindness, sleepiness, or distraction, could possibly keep us from discerning it! I have many a time wondered, that (as the eye is dazzled so with the beholding of the greatest light, that it can scarce perceive the shining of a lesser, so) the glorious transcendent majesty of the Lord, doth not even overwhelm our understandings, and so transport and take us up, as that we scarce observe or remember anything else. For naturally the greatest objects of our sense, are apt to make us at that time insensible of the smaller. And our exceeding great business, is apt to make us utterly neglect and forget those that are exceeding small. And O what nothings are the best and greatest of the creatures, in comparison of God! And what toys and trifles are all our other businesses in the world, in comparison of the business which we have with him! But I have been stopped in these admirations by considering that the wise Creator hath fitted and ordered all his creatures according to the use which he designeth them to. And therefore as the eye must be receptive only of so much light as is proportioned to its use and pleasure, and must be so distant from the sun, that its light may rather guide, than blind us, and its heat may rather quicken, than consume us; so God hath made our understandings capable of no other knowledge of him here, than what is suited to the work of holiness. And while we have flesh, and fleshly works to do, and lawful and necessary business in the world, which God's own commands employ us, our souls in this lantern of the body, must see him through so thick a glass, as shall so far allay our apprehension, as not to distract us, and take us off the works which he enjoineth us. And God and our souls shall be at such a distance, as that the proportionable light of his countenance may conduct us, and not overwhelm us; and his love may be so revealed, as to quicken our desires, and draw us on to a better state, but not so as to make us utterly impatient of this world and utterly weary of our lives, or to swallow us up, or possess us of our most desired happiness, before we arrive at the*state* of happiness. While the soul is in the body, it maketh so much use of the body (the brains and spirits) in all its operations; that our wise and merciful Creator and Governor, doth respect the body as well as the soul, in his ordering, disposing, and representing of the objects of those operations. So that when I consider that certainly all men would be distracted, if their apprehensions of God were any whit answerable to the greatness of his majesty and glory, (the brain being not able to bear such high operations of the soul, nor the greatness of the passions which would necessarily follow), it much reconcileth my wondering mind, to the wise and gracious providence of God, even in setting innocent nature itself at such a distance from his glory (allowing us the presence of such grace, as is necessary to bring us up to glory). Though it reconcile me not to that doleful distance which is introduced by sin, and which is furthered by Satan, the world, and the flesh, and which our Redeemer by his Spirit and intercession must heal.

And it further reconcileth me to this disposure and will of the blessed God, and this necessary natural distance and darkness of our mind, when I consider, that if God, and heaven, and hell, were as near and open to our apprehensions, as the things are which we see and feel, this life would not be what God intended it to be, a life of trial and preparation to another, a work, a race, a pilgrimage, a warfare; what trial would there be of any man's faith, or love, or obedience, or constancy, or self-denial? If we saw God stand by, or apprehended him as if we saw him (in degree) it would be no more praiseworthy or rewardable for a man to abhor all temptations to worldliness, ambition, gluttony, drunkenness, lust, cruelty, &c. than it is for a man to be kept from sleeping that is pierced with thorns, or for a man to forbear to drink a cup of melted gold which he knoweth will burn out his bowels, or to forbear to burn his flesh in fire. It were no great commendation to his chastity, that would forbear his filthiness, if he saw or had the fullest apprehensions of God; when he will forbear it in the presence of a mortal man. It were no great commendation to the intemperate and voluptuous, to have no mind of sensual delights, if they had but such a knowledge of God as were equal to sight. It were no thanks to the persecutor to forbear his cruelty against the servants of the Lord, if he "saw Christ coming with his glorious angels, to take vengeance on them that know not God, and obey not the Gospel, and to be admired in his saints, and glorified in them that now believe." (2 Thess. i. 7-10.) I deny not but this happily necessitated holiness is best in itself, and therefore will be our state in heaven; but what is there of trial in it? or how can it be suitable to the state of man, that must have good and evil set before him, and life and death left to his choice; and that must conquer if he will be crowned, and approve his fidelity to his Creator against competitors, and must live a rewardable life before he have the reward?

But though in this life we may neither hope for, nor desire, such overwhelming, sensible apprehensions of God, as the rest of our faculties cannot answer, nor our bodies bear; yet that our apprehensions of him should be so base, and small, and dull, and unconstant, as to be borne down by the noise of worldly business, or by the presence of any creature, or by the tempting baits of sensuality, this is the more odious, by how much God is more great and glorious than the creature, and even because the use of the creature itself is but to reveal the glory of the Lord. To have such slight and stupid thoughts of him, as will not carry us on in uprightness of obedience, nor keep us in his fear, nor draw out our hearts in sincere desires to please him, and enjoy him, and as will not raise us to a contempt of the pleasures, and profits, and honours of this world, this is to be despisers of the Lord, and to live as in a sleep, and to be dead to God, and alive only to the world and flesh. It is no unjust dishonour or injury to the creature, to be accounted as nothing in comparison of God, that it may be able to do nothing against him and his interest. But to make such a nothing of the most glorious God, by our contemptuous forgetfulness or neglect, as that our apprehensions of him cannot prevail against the sordid pleasures of the flesh, and against the richest baits of sin, and all the wrath or allurements of man, this is but to make a god of dust, and dung, and nothing, and (in heart and practice) to make God worse than dust and dung. And it is a wonder that man's understanding can become so sottish, as thus to wink the sun itself into a constant darkness, and to take God as nothing, or as no God, who is so abundantly revealed to them in astonishing transcendent greatness and excellency, by all the creatures in the world, and with whom we have continually so much to do. O sinful man! into how great a depth of ignorance, stupidity and misery art thou fallen!

But because we may see by the lives of the ungodly, that they little think that they have so much to do with God, though I have spoke of this to the godly in the other part of this treatise, I shall somewhat more particularly acquaint those that have most need to be informed of it, what business it is that they have with God.

1. It is not a business that may be done, or left undone like your business with men: but it is such as must be done, or you are undone forever. Nothing is absolutely necessary but this: nothing in all the world doth so much concern you. You may at far cheaper rates forbear to eat, or drink, or clothe yourselves, or live, than forbear the dispatch of this necessary work.

2. Your business with God, and for God in the world, is that which you have all your powers and endowments for; it is that which you were born into the world for, and that which you have understanding and freewill for, and that which you have your thoughts, and memories, and affections for, and that which you have eyes, and ears, and tongues, and your corporal parts and abilities for; and that which you have your time for; and your preservation, protection and provisions. It is that which you have all your teaching for; which Christ himself came into the world for; which the Scriptures are written for; which ministers are sent for; which all order and government in church and state is principally appointed for. In a word, it is that for which you have your lives, and all things, and without which all were as nothing, and will be to you worse than nothing, if they do not further your work with God. You will wish you had never seen them if they befriend you not in this.

3. Your business with God, and for him, is such as you must be continually doing: as is incumbent on you every hour, for you have every hour given you for this end. You may dispatch this man to day, and another tomorrow, and have no more to do with them again of a long time. But you have always incessantly important works to do with God. For your common work should be all his work; and all should be done with principal respect to him.

But I shall yet more particularly tell the ungodly what business it is that they have with God, which it seems, by their careless negligent lives, they are not aware of.

1. You must be either saved or damned by him; either glorified with him, or punished by him to everlasting: and it is now that the matter must be determined, which of the two conditions you must be in. You must now obtain your title to heaven, if ever you will come thither. You must now procure deliverance from hell-fire, if ever you will escape it. Now it is that all must be done, upon which

the scales must turn for your salvation or damnation: and you know this work is principally to be done between you and God, who alone can save you or destroy you; and yet do you forget him, and live as if you had no business with him, when you have your salvation to obtain from him, and your damnation to prevent! Have you such business as this with any other?

2. You have a strict and righteous judgment to undergo, in order to this salvation or damnation. You must stand before the Holy Majesty, and be judged by the Governor of the world: you must be there accused, and found guilty or not guilty; and judged as fulfillers, or as breakers of the holy covenant of grace. You must be set on the right hand or on the left. You must answer for all the time that you here spent, and for all the means and mercies which you here received, and for that you have done, whether it were good or evil. And it is now in this life that all your preparation must be made, and all that must be done, upon which your justification or condemnation will then depend. And it is between God and you that all this business must be done: and yet can you live as negligently towards him, as if you had no business with him?

3. You have a death to die, a change to make, which must be made but once; which will be the entrance upon endless joy or pain: and do you think this needeth not your most timely and diligent preparation? You must struggle with pains, and faint with weakness, and feel death taking down your earthen tabernacles. You must then have a life that is ending to review, and all that you have done laid open to your more impartial judgment; you must then see time as at an end, and the last sand running, and your candle ready to go out, and leave the snuff; you must then look back upon all that you had from the world, as ending; and upon all that you have done as that which cannot be undone again, that you may do it better; and you must have a more serious look into eternity, when you are stepping thither, than you can now conceive of. And doth all this need no preparation? It is with God that all that business must be now transacted, that must make your death to be comfortable or safe. If now you will only converse with men, and know no business that you have with God, you shall find at last to your exceeding terror, that you are in his hands, and passing to his bar, and that it is God that then you have to do with, when your business with all the world is at an end. He will then have something to do with you, if you will now find nothing to do with him.

4. In order to all this, you have now your peace to be made with God, and the pardon of all your sins to be obtained. For woe to you if then you are found under the guilt of any sin. Look back upon your lives, and remember how you have lived in the world, and what you have been doing: how you have spent your time in youth, and in your riper age; and how many sinful thoughts, and words, and deeds you have been guilty of; how oft you have sinfully pleased your appetites, and gratified your flesh, and yielded to temptations, and abused mercy, and lost your time. How oft you have neglected your duty, and betrayed your souls: how long you have lived in forgetfulness of God and your salvation; minding only the things of the flesh and of the world. How oft you have sinned ignorantly and against knowledge, through carelessness, and through rashness, through negligence and through presumption, in passion, and upon deliberation; against convictions, purposes and promises. How oft you have sinned against the precepts of piety to God, and of justice and charity to men. Think how your sins are multiplied and aggravated, more in number than the hours of your lives: aggravated by a world of mercies, by the clearest teachings and the loudest calls, and sharpest reproofs, and seasonable warnings, and by the long and urgent importunities of

grace. Think of all these, and then consider whether you have nothing now to do with God, whether it be not a business to be followed with all possible speed and diligence, to procure the pardon of all these sins. You have no such businesses as these to transact with men. You may have business with them which your estates depend upon, or which touch your credit, commodity or lives; but you have no business with men (unless in subordination to God) which your salvation doth depend upon. Your eternal happiness is not in their hands: they may kill your bodies (if God permit them), but not your souls. You need not solicit them to pardon your sins against God. It is a small matter how you are judged of by man. You have one that judgeth you, even the Lord. (1 Cor. iv. 3, 4.) No man can forgive sin, but God only. O then how early, how earnestly should you cry to him for mercy! Pardon must be obtained now or never. There is no justification for that man at the day of judgment, that is not forgiven and justified now. Blessed then is the man whose iniquity is forgiven, whose sin is covered, and to whom it is not imputed by the Lord. (Rom. iv. 7, 8.) And woe to that man that ever he was born, that is then found without the pardon of his sins! Think of this as the case deserves, and then think if you can, that your daily business with God is small.

5. Moreover, you have peace of conscience to obtain: and that dependeth upon your peace with God. Conscience will be your accuser, condemner and tormentor, if you make it not your friend, by making God your friend. Consider what conscience hath to say against you, and how certainly it will speak home, when you would be loath to hear it. And bethink you how to answer all its accusations, and what will be necessary to make it a messenger of peace; and then think your business with God to be but small, if you are able. It is no easy matter to get assurance that God is reconciled to you, and that he hath forgiven all your sins.

6. In order to all this, you must be united to Jesus Christ, and be made his members, that you may have part in him, and that he may wash you by his blood, and that he may answer for you to his Father! woe to you if he be not your righteousness, and if you have not him to plead your cause, and take upon him your final justification! None else can save you from the wrath of God. And he is the Saviour only of his body. (Ephes. v. 23.) He hath died for you without your own consent, and he hath made a universal conditional grant of pardon and salvation, before you consented to it: but he will not be united to you, nor actually forgive, and justify, and save you, without your own consent: and therefore that the Father may draw you to the Son, and may give you Christ, and life in him, (1 John v. 9-11), when all your hope dependeth on it, you may see that you have more to do with God, than your senseless hearts have hitherto understood.

7. And that you may have a saving interest in Jesus Christ, you must have sound repentance for all your former life of wickedness, and a lively, effectual faith in Christ: neither sin nor Christ must be made light of. Repentance must tell you to the very heart, that you have done foolishly in sinning, and that it is an evil and a bitter thing that you forsook the Lord, and that his fear was not in you: and thus your wickedness shall correct you and reprove you. (Jer. ii. 19.) And faith must tell you that Christ is more necessary to you than food or life, and that there is no other name given under heaven by which you can be saved. (Acts iv. 12.) And it is not so easy, nor so common a thing to repent and believe, as ignorant presumptuous sinners do imagine. It is a greater matter to have a truly humbled, contrite heart, and to loathe yourselves for all your sins, and to loathe those sins, and resolvedly give up yourselves to Christ and to his Spirit for a holy life, than heartlessly and hypocritically to say, I am sorry, or, I repent, without any true

contrition or renovation. And it is a greater matter to betake yourselves to Jesus Christ as your only hope, to save you both from sin and from damnation, than barely through custom, and the benefit of education, to say, I do believe in Christ. I tell you it is so great a work to bring you to sound repentance and faith, that it must be done by the power of God himself. (Acts v. 31; 2 Tim. ii. 25.) They are the "gift of God;" (Ephes. ii. 8.) you must have his Spirit to illuminate you, (Ephes. i. 18.), and show you the odiousness of sin, the intolerableness of the wrath of God, the necessity and sufficiency, the power and willingness of Christ; and to overcome all your prejudice, and save you from false opinions and deceits; and to repulse the temptations of Satan, the world and the flesh, which will all rise up against you. All this must be done to bring you home to Jesus Christ, or else you will have no part in him, his righteousness and grace. And can you think that you have not most important business with God, who must do all this upon you, or else you are undone forever!

8. Moreover you must have all the corruptions of your natures healed, and your sins subdued, and your hearts made new by sanctifying grace, and the image of God implanted in you, and your lives made holy and sincerely conformable to the will of God. All this must be done, or you cannot be acceptable to God, nor ever will be saved: though your carnal interest rise against it; though your old corrupted natures be against it; though your custom, and pleasure, and worldly gain and honour be against it; though all your carnal friends and superiors be against it; though the devil will do all that he can against it, yet all this must be done, or you are lost forever: and all this must be done by the Spirit of God; for it is his work to make you new and holy. And can you think then that the business is not great which you have with God? When you have tried how hard every part of this work is, to be begun and carried on, you will find you have more to do with God, than with all the world.

9. Moreover in order to this it is necessary that you read, and hear, and understand the Gospel, which must be the means of bringing you to God by Christ. This must be the instrument of God, by which he will bring you to repent and believe, and by which he will renew your natures, and imprint his image on you, and bring you to love him, and obey his will. The word of God must be your counsellor, and your delight, and you must set your heart to it, and meditate in it day and night. Knowledge must be the means to reclaim your perverse, misguided wills, and to reform your careless, crooked lives, and to bring you out of the kingdom of darkness, into the state of light and life. And such knowledge cannot be expected without a diligent attending unto Christ the teacher of your souls, and a due consideration of the truth. By that time you have learnt what is needful to be learnt for a true conversion, a sound repentance, a saving faith, and a holy life, you will find that you have far greater business with God than with all the world.

10. Moreover for the attaining of all this mercy, you have many a prayer to put up to God. You must daily pray for the forgiveness of your sins, and deliverance from temptations, and even for your daily bread, or necessary provisions for the work which you have to do: you must daily pray for the supplies of grace which you want, and for the gradual mortification of the flesh, and for help in all the duties which you must perform; and for strength against all spiritual enemies which will assault you; and preservation from the manifest evils which attend you: and these prayers must be put up with unwearied constancy, fervency and

faith. Keep up this course of fervent prayer, and beg for Christ, and grace, and pardon, and salvation in any measure as they deserve, and according to thy own necessity, and then tell me whether thy business with God be small, and to be put off as lightly as it is by the ungodly.

11. Moreover, you are made for the glory of your Creator, and must apply yourselves wholly to glorify him in the world: you must make his service the trade and business of your lives, and not put him off with something on the by. You are good for nothing else but to serve him; as a knife is made to cut, and as your clothes are made to cover you, and your meat to feed you, and your horse to labour for you; so you are made, and redeemed, and maintained for this, to love and please your great Creator. And can you think that it is but little business that you have with him, when he is the End and Master of your lives, and all you are or have is for him?

12. And for the due performance of his service, you have all his talents to employ. To this end it is that he hath entrusted you with reason, and health, and strength; with time, and parts, and interest, and wealth, and all his mercies, and all his ordinances and means of grace; and to this end must you use them, or you lose them: and you must give him an account of all at last, whether you have improved them all to your Master's use. And can you look within you, without you, about you, and see how much you are trusted with, and must be accountable to him for, and yet not see how great your business is with God?

13. Moreover, you have all the graces which you shall receive to exercise; and every grace doth carry you to God, and is exercised upon him, or for him. It is God that you must study, and know, and love, and desire, and trust, and hope in, and obey. It is God that you must seek after, and delight in, so far as you enjoy him. It is his absence or displeasure that must be your fear and sorrow: therefore the soul is said to be sanctified when it is renewed, because it is both disposed and devoted unto God. And therefore grace is called holiness, because it all disposeth, and carrieth the soul to God, and useth it upon and for him. And can you think your business with God is small, when you must live upon him, and all the powers of your soul must be addicted to him, and be in serious motion towards him? And when he must be much more to you than the air which you breathe in, or the earth you live upon, or than the sun that gives you light and heat; yea, than the soul is to your bodies?

14. Lastly, You have abundance of temptations and impediments to watch and strive against, which would hinder you in the doing of all this work, and a corrupt and treacherous heart to watch and keep in order, which will be looking back, and shrinking from the service. Lay all this together, and then consider whether you have not more and greater business with God, than with all the creatures in the world.

And if this be so (as undeniably it is so), is there any cloak for that man's sin, who is all day taken up with creatures, and thinks of God as seldom and as carelessly as if he had no business with him? And yet, alas, if you take a survey of high and low, of court, and city, and country, you shall find that this is the case of no small number, yea of many that observe it not to be their case; it is the case of the profane that pray in jest, and swear, and curse, and rail in earnest. It is the case of the malignant enemies of Holiness, that hate them at the heart that are most acquainted with this converse with God, and count it but hypocrisy, pride or fancy, and would not suffer them to live upon the earth, who are most sincerely conversant in heaven. It is the case of Pharisees and hypocrites, who take up with ceremonious observances, as, 'touch not, taste not, handle not,' and such like traditions of their forefathers, instead of a spiritual, rational service, and a holy, serious walking with the Lord. It is the case of all ambitious men, and covetous worldlings, who make more ado to climb up a little higher than their brethren, and to hold the reins, and have their wills, and be admired and adored in the world, or to get a large estate for themselves and their posterity, than to please their Maker, or to save their souls. It is the case of every sensual epicure, whose belly is his god, and serveth his fancy, lust and appetite before the Lord. It is the case of every unsanctified man, that seeketh first the prosperity of his flesh, before the kingdom and righteousness of God, and is most careful and laborious to lay up a treasure on earth, and laboureth more (with greater estimation, resolution, and delight), for the meat that perisheth, than for that which endureth to everlasting life. All these (who are too great a part of the world, and too great a part of professed Christians) are taken up with creature converse; and yet think to escape the deluge of God's displeasure, because the Enochs and Noahs are so few who walk with God; and they think God will not destroy so many: and thus they think to be saved by their multitude, and to hide themselves in the crowd from God. They will go the wide and common path, and be of the mind that most are of. They will not be convinced till most men are convinced; that is, till wisdom come too late, and cost them dearer than its worth. When all men are convinced that God should have been pre-ferred before the world, and served before their fleshly lusts (as they will certainly and sadly be), then they will be convinced with the rest. When all men understand that life was given them to have done the work which eternal life dependeth on, then they will understand it with the rest. When all men shall discern between the righteous and the wicked; between those that serve God, and that serve him not, then they will discern it with the rest. They will know what their business was in the world, and how much they had to do with God, when all men know it. But O how much better for them had it been to have known it in time, while knowledge might have done them better service, than to make them feel the greatness of their sin and folly, and the hopes which once they had of happiness, and to help the sting of desperation continually to prick them at the heart. They would not be of so "little a flock" as that to which it was the "good pleasure" of God to "give the kingdom." (Luke xii. 32.) If you demand a reason of all this, their reason was in their throats and bellies: they had fleshly appetites and lusts, and thereby could relish fleshly pleasures; but spiritual life and appetite they had none, and therefore relished not spiritual things. Had Christ, and holiness, and heaven, been as suitable to their appetites as the sweetness of their meat, and drink, and lusts, and as suitable to their fantasies as their worldly dignities and greatness were, they would then have made a better choice. They would have walked with God, if drunkenness, and gluttony, and pride, and wantonness, and covetousness, and idleness, had been the way in which they might have walked with him. If these had been godliness, how godly would they have been! How certainly would they have come to heaven if this had been the way! To be idle, and proud, and fleshly, and worldly, is it that they love; and to be humble, and holy, and heavenly, and mortified, is that which they hate, and cannot away with. And their love and ha-tred proceed from their corrupt natures; and these are instead of reason to them. Their strong apprehensions of a present suitableness in fleshly pleasures to their appetites, and of a present unsuitableness of a holy life, do keep out all effectual apprehensions of the excellencies of God, and of spiritual, heavenly delights, which cross them in the pleasures which they most desire.

But yet (their appetites corrupting their understandings as well as their wills) they will not be mad without some reason, nor reject their Maker and their happiness without some reason, nor neglect that holy work which they were made for without some reason. Let us hear then what it is.

Chapter III.

Object. 1. They say, 'It is true that God hath much to do with us, and for us. But it followeth not that we have so much to do with him, or for him, as you would have us to believe: for he is necessarily good, and necessarily doth good; and therefore will do so, whether we think of him or not. The sun will not give over shining on me, though I never think on it, or never pray to it, or give it thanks. Nor doth God need any service, that we can do him, no more than the sun doth; nor is he pleased any more in the praise of men, or in their works.'

Answ. 1. It is most certain that God is good as necessarily as he is God. But it is not true, that he must necessarily do good to you, or other individual persons; nor that he necessarily doth the good he doth them. As he is not necessitated to make toads and serpents as happy as men, of men as angels; so he is not necessitated to save the devils or damned souls (for he will not save them). And he was under, no greater a necessity to save you, than them. He was not necessitated to give you a being; he could have passed you by, and caused others to have possessed your room. As it was God's freewill, and not any necessity, that millions more are never born, that were in possibility of it: (for all that is possible doth not come to pass). So that you and millions more were born was not of necessity but of the same freewill. And as God did not make you of necessity but of freewill; so he doth not necessarily but freely justify, or sanctify, or save. If he did it by necessity of nature, he would do it to all as well as some; seeing all have a natural capacity of grace as well as those that receive it. God is able to sanctify and save more, yea all, if it were his will: and it is not for want of power or goodness that he doth not. Millions of beings are possible which are not future. God doth not all the good which he is able, but communicateth so much to his several creatures as to his wisdom seemeth meet. If the damned would be so presumptuous as to argue, that because God is able yet to sanctify and save them, therefore he must do it of necessity of nature, it would not be long before they should thus dispute themselves out of their torments. God will not ask leave of sinners to be God: their denying him to be good (that is to be God), because he complieth not with their conceits and wills, doth but prove them to be fools and bad themselves.

Indeed some sciolists, pretending to learning, while they are ignorant of most obvious principles of natural knowledge, have taught poor sinners to cheat their souls with such dreams as these. They have made themselves believe that goodness in God is nothing else but his benignity, or disposition to do good. As if the creature were the ultimate end, and all God's goodness but a means thereto. And so God were the Alpha or first efficient, and yet the creature the Omega or 'finis ultimus:' and all the goodness in God were to be estimated and denominated by its respect to the felicity of man: and so the creature hath the best part of the Deity. Such notions evidently show us, that lapsed man is predominantly selfish, and is become his own idol, and is lost in himself, while he hath lost himself by his loss of God. When we see how powerful his self-interest is, both with his intellect and will; even men of great ingenuity, till sanctification hath restored them to God, and taught them better to know him and themselves, are ready to measure all good or evil by their own interests; when yet common reason would have told them, if they had not perverted it by pride and partial studies, that short of God, even among the creatures, there are many things to be preferred before themselves and their own felicity. He is irrationally enslaved by self-love, that cannot see that the happiness of the world, or of his country, or of multitudes, is more to be desired than his happiness alone: and that he ought rather to choose to be annihilated, or to be miserable (if it were made a matter of his deliberation and choice), than to have the sun taken out of the firmament, or the world, or his country to be annihilated or miserable. And God is infinitely above the creature.

Object. But they say, 'He needeth nothing to make him happy, having no defect of happiness.'

Answ. And what of that? Must it needs therefore follow, that he made not all things for himself, but for the creature finally? He is perfectly happy in himself, and his will is himself: this will was fulfilled when the world was not made (for it was his will that it should not be made till it was made), and it is fulfilled when it is made, and fulfilled by all that comes to pass. And as the absolute simple goodness and perfection of God's essence is the greatest good, the eternal immutable good; so the fulfilling of his will is the ultimate end of all obedience. He hath expressed himself to take pleasure in his works, and in the holiness, obedience and happiness of his chosen: and though pleasure be not the same thing in God as it is in a man (no more than will or understanding is), yet it is not nothing which God expresseth by such terms, but something which we have no fitter expression for: this pleasing of the will of God being the end of all, even of our felicity, is better than our felicity itself.

They that will maintain that God, who is naturally and necessarily good, hath no other goodness but his benignity, or aptness to do good to his creatures, must needs also maintain that (God being, for the creature, and not the creature for God) the creature is better than God, as being the ultimate end of God himself, and the highest use of all his goodness being but for the felicity of the creature. As also that God doth all the good that he is able: (for natural necessary agents work 'ad ultimum posse'). And that all men shall be saved, and all devils, and every worm and toad be equal to the highest angel, or else that God is not able to do it. And that he did thus make happy all his creatures from eternity (for natural, necessary agents work always if they be not forcibly hindered); and that there never was such a thing as pain or misery, in man or brute, or else that God was not able to prevent it. But abundance of such odious consequences must needs follow from the denying of the highest Good, which is God himself, and confessing none but his efficient goodness. But some will be offended with me for being so serious in confuting such an irrational, atheistical conceit, who know not how far it prevaileth with an atheistical generation.

Be it known to you, careless sinners, that though the sun will shine on you whether you think on it or not, or love it, or thank it or not; and the fire will warm you whether you think on it or not, or love it or not; yet God will not justify or save you, whether you love him or think on him or not. God doth not operate brutishly in your salvation; but governeth you wisely, as rational creatures are to be governed; and therefore will give you happiness as a reward; and therefore will not deal alike with those that love him, and that love him not; that seek him and that seek him not; with the labourers and the loiterers, the faithful and slothful servant. Would you have us believe that you know better than God himself what pleaseth himself, or on what terms he will give his benefits, and save men's souls? Or do you know his nature better than he knoweth it, that you dare presume to say, because he needeth not our love or duty, therefore they are not pleasing to him! Then what hath God to do in governing the world, if he be pleased and displeased with nothing that men do, or with good and evil actions equally? Though you cannot hurt him, you shall find that he will hurt you, if you disobey him. And though you cannot make him happy by your holiness, you shall find that he will not make you happy without it.

And if he did work as necessarily as the sun doth shine, according to your similitude; yet, 1. Even the shining of the sun doth not illuminate the blind, nor doth it make the seeds of thorns and nettles to bring forth vines or roses, nor the gendering of frogs to bring forth men; but it actuateth all things according to the several natures of their powers. And therefore how can you expect that an unbelieving and unholy soul, should enjoy felicity in God, when in that state they are incapable of it? 2. And if the sun do necessarily illuminate anyone, he must necessarily be illuminated; and if it necessarily warm or quicken anything, it must necessarily be warmed and quickened; else you would assert contradictions. So if God did necessarily save you, and make you happy, you would necessarily be saved and made happy. And that containeth essentially your holiness, your loving, desiring and seeking after God; to be saved or happy without enjoying God by love, or to love him and not desire him, seek him or obey him, are as great contradictions as to be illuminated without light, or quickened without life. What way soever it be that God conveyeth his sanctifying Spirit, I am sure that "if any man have not the Spirit of Christ, the same is none of his," (Rom. viii. 9.), and that without "holiness none shall see God," (Heb. xii. 14.), and that if you will have the kingdom of God, you must seek it first, preferring it before all earthly things. (Matt. vi. 33.; John vi. 27; Col. iv. 1-3.) And then if all the question that remaineth undecided be, whether God do you wrong or not in damning you, or whether God be good because he will not save you when he can, I shall leave you to him to receive satisfaction, who will easily silence and confound your impudence, and justify his works and laws. Prepare your accusations against him, if you will needs insist upon them, and try whether he or you shall prevail: but remember that thou art a worm, and he is God, and that he will be the only Judge when all is done; and ignorance and impiety, that prate against him to their own confusion, in the day of his patience, shall not then usurp the throne.

Object. 2. 'But how can God be fit for mortals to converse with, when they see him not, and are infinitely below him?'

Answ. I hope you will not say that you have nothing to do at home, with your own souls: and yet you never saw your souls. And it is the souls, the reason and the will of men that you daily converse with here in the world, more than their bodies, and yet you never saw their souls, their reason or their wills. If you have no higher light to discern by than your eyesight, you are not men but beasts. If you are men, you have reason; and if you are Christians, you have faith, by which you know things that you never saw. You have more dependence on the things that are unseen, than on those which you see, and have much more to do with them.

And though God be infinitely above us; yet he condescendeth to communicate to us according to our capacities. As the sun is far from us, and yet doth not disdain to enlighten, and warm, and quicken a worm or fly here below. If any be yet so much an atheist as to think that religious converse with God is but a fancy, let him well answer me these few questions.

Quest. 1. Doth not the continued being and well-being of the creatures, tell us that there is a God on whom (for being and well-being) they depend, and from whom they are and have whatsoever they are, and whatsoever they have? And therefore that passively all the creatures have more respect to him by far, than to one another?

Quest. 2. Seeing God communicateth to every creature according to their several capacities; is it not meet then that he deal with man as man, even as a creature rational, capable to know, and love, and obey his great Creator, and to be happy in the knowledge, love and fruition of him? That man hath such natural faculties, and capacities, is not to be denied by a man that knoweth what it is to be a man. And that God hath not given him these in vain, will be easily believed by any that indeed believe that he is God.

Quest. 3. Is there anything else that is finally worthy of the highest actions of our souls or that is fully adequate to them, and fit to be our happiness? If not, then we are left either to certain infelicity, contrary to the tendency of our natures, or else we must seek our felicity in God.

Quest. 4. Is there anything more certain than that by the title of creation, our Maker hath a full and absolute right to all that he hath made; and consequently to all our love and obedience, our time and powers? For whom should they all be used but for him from whom we have them?

Quest. 5. Can anything be more sure, than that God is the righteous Governor of the world? And that he governeth man as a rational creature, by laws and judgment? And can we live under his absolute sovereignty, and under his many righteous laws, and under his promises of salvation to the justified, and under his threatenings of damnation to the unjustified, and yet not have more to do with God than with all the world? If indeed you think that God doth not love and reward the holy and obedient, and punish the ungodly and disobedient, then either you take him not to be the Governor of the world, or (which is worse) you take him to be an unrighteous Governor. And then you must by the same reason say, that magistrates and parents should do so too, and love and reward the obedient and disobedient alike. But if any man's disobedience were exercised to your hurt, by slandering, or beating, or robbing you, I dare say you would not then commend so indifferent and unjust a Governor.

Quest. 6. If it be not needless for man to labour for food and raiment, and necessary provision for his body, how can it be needless for him to labour for the happiness of his soul? If God will not give us our daily bread while we never think of it, or seek it, why should we expect that he will give us heaven though we never think on it, value it, or seek it?

Quest. 7. Is it not a contradiction to be happy in the fruition of God, and yet not to mind him, desire him, or seek him? How is it that the soul can reach its object, but by estimation, desire and seeking after it. And how should it enjoy it but by loving it, and taking pleasure in it?

Quest. 8. While you seem but to wrangle against the duty of believers, do you not plead against the comfort and happiness of believers? For surely the employment of the soul on God (and for him) is the health and pleasure of the soul; and to call away the soul from such employment, is to imprison it in the dungeon of this world, and to forbid us to smell to the sweetest flowers, and confine us to a sink or dunghill, and to forbid us to taste of the food of angels, or of men, and to offer us vinegar and gall, or turn us over to feed with swine. He that pleadeth that there is no such thing as real holiness and communion with God, doth plead in effect that there is no true felicity or delight for any of the sons of men. And how welcome should ungodly atheists be unto mankind, that would forever exclude them all from happiness, and make them believe they are all made to be remedilessly miserable?

And here take notice of the madness of the unthankful world, that hateth and persecuteth the preachers of the Gospel, that bring them the glad tidings of pardon, and hope, and life eternal, of solid happiness, and durable delight; and yet they are not offended at these atheists and ungodly cavillers, that would take them off from all that is truly good and pleasant, and make them believe that nature hath made them capable of no higher things than beasts, and hath enthralled them in remediless infelicity.

Quest. 9. Do you not see by experience that there are a people in the world whose hearts are upon God, and the life to come, and that make it their chiefest care and business to seek him and to serve him? How then can you say that there is no such thing, or that we are not capable of it, when it is the case of so many before your eyes? If you say that it is but their fancy or self-deceit. I answer, That really their hearts are set upon God, and the everlasting world, and that it is their chiefest care and business to attain it; this is a thing that they feel, and you may see in the bent and labour of their lives; and therefore you cannot call that a fancy, of which you have so full experience. But whether the motives that have invited them, and engaged them to such a choice and course, be fancies and deceits or not, let God be judge, and let the awakened consciences of worldlings themselves be judge, when they have seen the end, and tried whether it be earth or heaven that is the shadow, and whether it be God or their unbelieving hearts that was deceived.

Quest. 10. Have you any hopes of living with God forever, or not? If you have not, no wonder if you live as beasts, when you have no higher expectations than beasts. When we are so blind as to give up all our hopes, we will also give up all our care and holy diligence, and think we have nothing to do with heaven. But if you have any such hopes, can you think that anything is fitter for the chiefest of your thoughts and cares, than the God and kingdom, which you hope forever to enjoy? Or is there anything that can be more suitable, or should be more delightful to your thoughts, than to employ them about your highest hopes, upon your endless happiness and joy? And should not that be now the most noble and pleasant employment for your minds, which is nearest to that which you hope to be exercised in forever? Undoubtedly he that hath true and serious thoughts of heaven, will most highly value that life on earth which is most like to the life in heaven. And he that hateth, or is most averse to that which is nearest to the work of heaven, does boast in vain of his hopes of heaven.

By this time you may see (if you love not to be blind) that man's chiefest business in the world is with his God, and that our thoughts, and all our powers, are made to be employed upon him, or for him; and that this is no such needless work as atheists make themselves believe.

Remember that it is the description of the desperately wicked, (Psal.x.iv.), that "God is not in all their thoughts." And if yet you understand it not, I will a little further show you the evil of such atheistical, unhallowed thoughts.

1. There is nothing but darkness in all thy thoughts, if God be not in them. Thou knowest nothing, if thou knowest not him; and thou usest not thy knowledge, if thou use it not on him. To know the creature as without God, is to know

nothing: no more than to know all the letters in the book, and not to know their signification or sense. All things in the world are but insignificant ciphers, and of no other sense or use, if you separate them from God, who is their sense and end. If you leave out God in all your studies, you do but dream and doat, and not understand what you seem to understand. Though you were taken for the most learned men in the world, and were able to discourse of all the sciences, and your thoughts had no lower employment daily than the most sublime speculations which the nature of all the creatures doth afford, it is all but folly and impertinent dotage, if it reach not unto God.

2. Yea, your thoughts are erroneous and false, which is more than barely ignorant, if God be not in them. You have false thoughts of the world, of your houses and lands, and friends and pleasures, and whatsoever is the daily employment of your minds. You take them to be something, when they are nothing; you are covetous of the empty purse, and know not that you cast away the treasure. You are thirsty after the empty cup, when you willfully cast away the drink. You hungrily seek to feed upon a painted feast. You murder the creature by separating it from God who is its life, and then you are enamoured on the carcass; and spend your days and thoughts in its cold embracements. Your thoughts are but vagabonds, straggling abroad the world, and following impertinencies, if God be not in them. You are like men that walk up and down in their sleep, or like those that have lost themselves in the dark, who weary themselves in going they know not whither, and have no end nor certain way.

3. If God be not in all your thoughts, they are all in vain. They are like the drone that gathereth no honey. They fly abroad and return home empty. They bring home no matter of honour to God, or profit or comfort to yourselves. They are employed to no more purpose than in your dreams: only they are more capable of sin: like the distracted thoughts of one that doteth in a fever, they are all but nonsense, whatever you employ them on, while you leave out God, who is the sense of all.

4. If God be not in all your thoughts, they are nothing but confusion. There can be no just unity in them, because they forsake him who is the only centre, and are scattered abroad upon incoherent creatures. There can be no true unity but in God. The further we go from him, the further we run into divisions and confusions. There can be no just method in them, because he is left out that is the beginning and the end. They are not like a well-ordered army, where everyone is moved by the will of one commander, and all know their colours and their ranks, and unanimously agree to do their work. But like a swarm of flies, that buzz about they know not whither, nor why, nor for what. There is no true government in your thoughts, if God be not in them; they are masterless and vagrants, and have no true order, if they be not ordered by him and to him; if he be not their first and last.

5. If God be not in all your thoughts, there is no life in them: they are but like the motion of a bubble, or a feather in the air: they are impotent as to the resisting of any evil, and as to the doing of any saving good: they have no strength in them, because they are laid out upon objects that have no strength: they have no quickening, renewing, reforming, encouraging, resolving, confirming power in them, because there is no such power in the things on which they are employed: whereas the thoughts of God and everlasting life, can do wonders upon the soul: they can raise up men above this world, and teach them to despise the worldling's idol, and look upon all the pleasures of the flesh as upon a swine's delight in wallowing in

the mire. They can renew the soul, and cast out the most powerful beloved sin, and bring all our powers into the obedience of God, and that with pleasure and delight: they can employ us with the angels, in a heavenly conversation, and show us the glory of the world above, and advance us above the life of the greatest princes upon earth: but the thoughts of earthly, fleshly things have power indeed to delude men, and mislead them, and hurry them about in a vertiginous motion; but no power to support us, or subdue concupiscence, or heal our folly, or save us from temptations, or reduce us from our errors, or help us to be useful in the world, or to attain felicity at last. There is no life, nor power, nor efficacy in our thoughts, if God be not in them.

6. There is no stability or fixedness in our thoughts if God be not in them. They are like a boat upon the ocean, tossed up and down with winds and waves: the mutable uncertain creatures can yield no rest or settlement to your minds. You are troubled about many, things; and the more you think on them, and have to do with them, the more are you troubled: but you forget the one thing necessary, and fly from the eternal rock, on which you must build, if ever you will be established. While the creature is in your thought instead of God, you will be one day deluded with its unwholesome pleasure, and the next day feel it gripe you at the heart: one day it will seem your happiness, and the next you will wish you had never known it: that which seemeth the only comfort of your lives this year, may the next year make you weary of your lives. One day you are impatiently desiring and seeking it, as if you could not live without it: and the next day, or ere long you are impatiently desiring to be rid of it. You are now taking in your pleasant morsels, and drinking down your delicious draughts, and jovially sporting it with your inconsiderate companions; but how quickly will you be repenting of all this, and complaining of your folly, and vexing yourselves, that you took not warning, and made not a wiser choice in time? The creature was never made to be our end, or rest, or happiness: and therefore you are but like a man in a wilderness or maze, that may go and go, but knoweth not whither, and findeth no end, till you come home to God, who only is your proper end, and make him the Lord, and life, and pleasure of your thoughts.

7. As there is no present fixedness in your thoughts, so the business and pleasure of them will be of very short continuance, if God be not the chief in all. And who would choose to employ his thoughts on such things as he is sure they must soon forget, and never more have any business with to all eternity? You shall think of those houses, and lands, and friends, and pleasures, but a little while, unless it be with repenting, tormenting thoughts, in the place of misery: you will have no delight to think of anything, which is now most precious to your flesh, when once the flesh itself decays, and is no more capable of delight. "His breath goeth forth, he returneth to his earth; in that very day his thoughts perish." (Psal. cxlvi. 4.)

Call in your thoughts then from these transitory things, that have no consistency or continuance, and turn them unto him with whom they may find everlasting employment and delight. Remember not the enticing baits of sensuality and pride, but "Remember now thy Creator in the days of thy youth, while the evil days come not, nor the years draw nigh, when thou shalt say, I have no pleasure in them."

8. Thy thoughts are but sordid, dishonourable and low, if God be not the chiefest in them. They reach no higher than the habitation of beasts; nor do they attain to any sweeter employment than to meditate on the, felicity of a brute.

Thou choosest with the fly to feed on dung and filthy ulcers, and as maggots to live on stinking carrion, when thou mightest have free access to God himself, and mightest be entertained in the court, of heaven, and welcomed thither by the holy angels. Thou wallowest in the mire with the swine, or diggest thyself a house in the earth, as worms and moles, do, when thy thoughts might be soaring up to God, and might be taken up with high and holy, and everlasting things. What if your thoughts were employed for preferment, wealth, and honour in the world? Alas! what silly things are these, in comparison of what your souls are capable of! You will say so yourselves when you see how they will end, and fail your expectations. Imprison not your minds in this infernal cell, when the superior regions are open to their access: confine them not to this narrow vessel of the body, whose tossings and dangers on these boisterous seas will make them restless, and disquiet them with tumultuous passions, when they may safely land in Paradise, and there converse with Christ. God made you men, and if you reject not his grace, will make your saints: make not yourselves like beasts or vermin. God gave you souls that can step in a moment from earth to heaven, and there foretaste the endless joys: do not you stick then fast in clay, and fetter them with worldly cares, or intoxicate them with fleshly pleasures, nor employ them in the worse than childish toys of ambitious, sensual, worldly men. Your thoughts have manna, angels' food, provided them by God: if you will loathe this and refuse it, and choose with the serpent to feed on the dust, or upon the filth of sin, God shall be judge, and your consciences one day shall be more faithful witnesses, whether you have dealt like wise men or like fools; like friends or enemies to yourselves; and whether you have not chosen baseness, and denied yourselves the advancement which was offered you.

9. If God be not the chiefest in your thoughts, they are no better than dishonest and unjust. You are guilty of denying him his own. He made not your minds for lust and pleasure, but for himself. You expect that your cattle, your goods, your servants, be employed for yourselves, because they are your own. But God may call your minds his own by a much fuller title: for you hold all but derivatively and dependently from him. What will you call it but injustice and dishonesty, if your wife, or children, or servants, or goods, be more at the use and service of others, than of you? If any can show a better title to your thoughts than God doth, let him have them; but if not, deny him not his own. O straggle not so much from home; for you will be nowhere else so well as there. Desire not to follow strangers, you know not whither, nor for what; you have a Master of your own, that will be better to you than all the strangers in the world. Bow not down to creatures, that are but images of the true and solid good: commit not idolatry or adultery with them in your thoughts: remember still that God stands by: bethink you how he will take it at your hands; and how it will be judged of at last, when he pleads his right, his kindness, and solicitations of you; and you have so little to say for any pretence of right or merit in the creature. Why are not men ashamed of the greatest dishonesty against God, when all that have any humility left them, do take adultery, theft, and other dishonesty against creatures, for a shame? The time will come when God and his interest shall be better understood, when this dishonesty against him, will be the matter of the most confounding shame, that ever did or could befall men. Prevent this by the juster exercise of your thoughts, and keeping them pure and chaste to God.

10. If God be not in your thoughts (and the chiefest in them) there will be no matter in them of solid comfort or content. Trouble and deceit will be all their

work: when they have fled about the earth, and taken a taste of every flower, they will come loaden home with nothing better than vanity and vexation. Such thoughts may excite the laughter of a fool, and cause that mirth that is called madness; (Eccles. vii. 4. 6; ii. 2.); but they will never conduce to settled peace, and durable content, and therefore they are always repented of themselves, and are troublesome to our review, as being the shame of the sinner, which he would fain be cleared of, or disown. Though you may approach the creature with passionate fondness and the most delightful promises and hopes, be sure of it, you will come off at last with grief and disappointment, if not with the loathing of that which you chose for your delight. Your thoughts are in a wilderness among thorns and briars, when God is not in them as their guide and end: they are lost and torn among the creatures; but rest and satisfaction they will find none. It may be at the present it is pleasanter to you to think of recreation, or business, or worldly wealth, than to think of God; but the pleasure of these thoughts is as delusory, and short-lived, as are the things themselves on which you think. How long will you think with pleasure on such fading transitory things? And the pleasure cannot be greater at the present, which reacheth but the flesh and fantasy, and which the possessed knoweth will be but short.

Nay, you will shortly find by sad experience, that of all the creatures under heaven, there will none be so bitter to your thoughts, as those which you now find greatest carnal sweetness in. O how bitter will the thought of idolized honour, and abused wealth and greatness be, to a dying or a damned Dives! The thoughts of that alehouse or playhouse where thou hadst thy greatest pleasure, will trouble thee more than the thoughts of all the houses in the town besides! The thoughts of that one woman with whom thou didst commit thy pleasant sin, will wound and vex thee more than the thoughts of all the women in the town besides! The thoughts of that beloved sport which thou couldst not be weaned from, will be more troublesome to thee than the thoughts of a thousand other things in which thou hadst no inordinate delight! For the end of sinful mirth is sorrow. When Solomon had tried to please himself to the full, in mirth, in buildings, vineyards, woods, waters, in servants, and possessions, silver, and gold, and cattle, and singers, and instruments of music of all sorts, in greatness, and all that the eye or appetite or heart desired; he findeth when he awaked from this pleasant dream, that he had all this while been taken up with vanity and vexation, in so much that he saith on the review, "Therefore I hated life, because the work that is wrought under the sun, is grievous to me, for all is vanity and vexation of spirit. Yea, I hated all my labour which I had taken under the sun." (Eccles. ii. 1-3, &c.; xvii. 18.) You may toil out and tire yourselves among these briars, in this barren wilderness; but if ever you would feel any solid ground of quietness and rest, it must be by coming off from vanity, and seeking your felicity in God, and living sincerely for him and upon him, as the worldling doth upon the world. His pardoning mercy must begin your peace, forgiving you your former thoughts; and his healing, quickening mercy must increase it, by teaching you better to employ your thoughts, and drawing up your hearts unto himself; and his glorifying mercy must perfect it, by giving you the full intuition and fruition of himself in heaven, and employing you in his perfect love and praise, not leaving any room for creatures, nor suffering a thought to be employed on vanity forever.

CHAPTER IV.

By this time I hope you may see reason to call yourselves to a strict account, what converse you have been taken up with in the world, and upon what you have exercised your thoughts. Surely you must needs be conscious, that the thoughts which have been denied God, have brought you home but little satisfaction, and have not answered the ends of your creation, redemption or preservation, and that they are now much fitter matter for your penitential tears, than your comfort, in the review! I do not think you dare own, and stand to those thoughts which have been spent for fleshly pleasures, or in unnecessary worldly cares, or that were wasted in impertinent vagaries upon anything, or nothing, when you should have been seeking God! I do not think you have now any great pleasure, in the review of those thoughts, which once were taken up with pleasure, when your most pleasant thoughts should have been of God. Dare you approve of your rejecting your Creator, and the great concernments of your soul, out of your thoughts, and wasting them upon things unprofitable and vain? Did not God and heaven deserve more of your serious thoughts than anything else that ever they were employed on? Have you laid them out on anything that more concerned you? Or on anything more excellent, more honourable, more durable, or that could claim precedency upon any just account? Did you not shut heaven itself out of your thoughts, when you shut out God? And is it not just that God and heaven should shut out you? If heaven be not the principal matter of your thoughts, it is plain that you do not principally love it: and if so, judge you whether those that love it not are fit to be made possessors of it.

O poor distracted senseless world! Is not God great enough to command and take up your chiefest thoughts? Is not heaven enough to find them work, and afford them satisfaction and delight? And yet is the dung and dotage of the world enough? Is your honour, and wealth, and fleshly delights, and sports enough? God will shortly make you know, whether this were wise and equal dealing! Is God so low, so little, so undeserving, to be so oft and easily forgotten, and so hardly, and so slightly remembered? I tell you, ere long he will make you think of him to your sorrow, whether you will or no, if grace do not now set open your hearts, and procure him better entertainment.

But perhaps you will think that you walk with God, because you think of him sometimes ineffectually, and as on the by. But is he esteemed as your God, if he have not the command, and if he have not the precedency of his creatures? Can you dream that indeed you walk with God, when your hearts were never grieved for offending him, nor never much solicitous how to be reconciled to him; nor much inquisitive whether your state or way be pleasing or displeasing to him? When all the business of an unspeakable importance, which you have to do with God, before you pass to judgment, is forgotten and undone, as if you knew not of any such work that you had to do! When you make no serious preparation for death, when you call not upon God in secret, or in your families, unless with a little heartless lip labour; and when you love not the spirituality of his worship, but only delude your souls with the mockage of hypocritical outside compliment. Do you walk with God while you are plotting for preferment, and gaping after worldly greatness; while you are gratifying all the desires of your flesh, and making provision for the future satisfaction of its lusts? (Rom. xiii. 13.) Are you walking with God when you are hating him in his holiness, his justice, his word and ways, and hating all that seriously love and seek him; when you are doing your worst to dispatch the work of your damnation, and put your salvation past all hope, and draw as many to hell with you as you can? If this be a walking with God, you may take further comfort that you shall also dwell with God, according to the sense of such a walk: you shall dwell with him as a devouring fire, and as just, whom you thus walked with in the contempt of his mercies, and the provocation of his justice.

I tell you, if you walked with God indeed, his authority would rule you, his greatness would much take up your minds, and leave less room for little things; you would trust his promises, and fear his threatenings, and be awed by his presence, and the idols of your hearts would fall before him: he would overpower your lusts, and call you off from your ambitious and covetous designs, and obscure all the creature's glory. Believing, serious, effectual thoughts of God, are very much different from the common, doubtful, dreaming, ineffectual thoughts of the ungodly world.

Object. But (perhaps some will say), 'This seemeth to be the work of preachers, and not of every Christian to be always meditating of God: poor people must think of other matters: they have their business to do, and their families to provide for: and ignorant people are weak-headed, and are not able either to manage or endure a contemplative life. So much thinking of God will make them melancholy and mad, as experience tells us it hath done by many: and therefore this is no exercise for them.'

To this I answer, 1. Every Christian hath a God to serve, and a soul to save, and a Christ to believe in and obey, and an endless happiness to secure and enjoy, as well as preachers. Pastors must study to instruct their flock, and to save themselves, and those that hear them. The people must study to understand and receive the mercy offered them, and to make their calling and election sure. It is not said of pastors only, but of every blessed man, that "his delight is in the law of the Lord, and therein doth he meditate day and night." (Psal. i. 2.) 2. And the due meditation of the soul upon God, is so far from taking you off from your necessary business in the world, that it is the only way to your orderly and successful management of it. 3. And it is not a distracting thoughtfulness that I persuade you to, or which is included in a Christian's walk with God; but it is a directing, quickening, exalting, comforting course of meditation. Many a hundred have grown melancholy and mad with careful, discontented thoughts of the world; it doth not follow therefore that no man must think of the world at all, for fear of being mad or melancholy; but only that they should think of it more regularly, and correct the error of their thoughts and passions. So is it about God and heavenly things. Our thoughts are to be well ordered, and the error of them cured, and not the use of them forborne. Atheism and impiety, and forgetting God, are unhappy means to prevent melancholy. There are wiser means for avoiding madness, than by renouncing all our reason, and living by sense, like the beasts that perish, and forgetting that we have an everlasting life to live.

But yet because I am sensible that some do here mistake on the other hand,

and I would not lead you into any extreme, I shall fully remove the scruple contained in this objection, by showing you in the following propositions, in what sense, and how far your thoughts must be taken up with God (supposing what was said in the beginning, where I described to you the duty of walking with God).

Prop. 1. When we tell you that your thoughts must be on God, it is not a course of idle musing, or mere thinking, that we call you to, but it is a necessary practical thinking of that which you have to do, and of him that you must love, obey and enjoy. You will not forget your parents, or husband, or wife, or friend; and yet you will not spend your time in sitting still and thinking of them, with a musing unprofitable thoughtfulness. But you will have such thoughts of them, and so many as are necessary to the ends, even to the love and service which you owe them, and to the delight that your hearts should have in the fruition of them. You cannot love, or obey, or take pleasure in those that you will not think of. You will follow your trades, or your master's service but unhappily, if you will not think on them. Thinking is not the work that we must take up with: it is but a subservient, instrumental duty, to promote some greater, higher duty: therefore we must think of God, that we may love him, and do his service, and trust him, and fear, and hope in him, and make him our delight. And all this is it that we call you to, when we are persuading you to think on God.

2. An hypocrite, or a wicked enemy of God, may think of him speculatively, and perhaps be more frequent in such thoughts than many practical believers. A learned man may study about God, as he doth about other matters, and names, and notions; and propositions and decisions concerning God, may be a principal part of his learning. A preacher may study about God, and the matters of God, as a physician or a lawyer does about matters of their own profession, either for the pleasure which knowledge, as knowledge, brings to human nature, or for the credit of being esteemed wise and learned, or because their gain and maintenance comes in this way. They that fill many volumes with controversies concerning God, and fill the church with contentions and troubles by them, and their own heart with malice and uncharitableness against those that are not of their opinions, have many and many a thought of God, which yet will do nothing to the Saving of their souls, no more than they do to the sanctifying of them. And such learned men may think more orthodoxly and methodically concerning God, than many an honest, serious Christian, who yet thinks of him more effectually and savingly: even as they can discourse more orderly and copiously of God, when yet they have no saving knowledge of him.

3. All men must not bestow so much time in meditation as some must do: it is the calling of ministers to study so as to furnish their minds with all those truths concerning God, which are needful to the edification of the church; and so to meditate on these things as to give themselves wholly to them. (1 Tim. iv. 15, 16.) It is both the work of their common and their special calling. The study necessary to Christians as such, belongeth as well to others as to them: but other men have another special or particular calling, which also they must think of, so far as the nature and ends of their daily labours do require. It is a hurtful error to imagine that men must either lay by their callings to meditate on God, or that they must do them negligently, or to be taken up in the midst of their employments with such studies of God as ministers are, that are separated to that work.

4. No man is bound to be continually taken up with actual, distinct thoughts of God: for in duty we have many other things to think on, which must have their time: and as we have callings to follow, and must eat our bread in the sweat of

our brows, so we must manage them with prudence: "A good man will guide his affairs with discretion." (Psal. cxii. 5.) It is both necessary as a duty, and necessary as a means to the preservation of our very faculties, that both body and mind have their times of employment about our lawful business in the world. The understandings of many cannot bear it, to be always employed on the greatest and most serious things. Like lute strings they will break, if they be raised too high, and be not let down and relaxed, when the lesson is played. To think of nothing else but God, is to break the law of God, and to confound the mind, and to disable it to think aright of God, or anything. As he that bid us pray continually, did not mean that we should do nothing else, or that actual prayer should have no interruptions, but that habitual desires should on all meet occasions be actuated and expressed; so he that would be chief in all their thoughts, did never mean that we should have no thoughts of anything else, or that our serious meditation on him should be continual without interruption; but that the final intending of God, and our dependence on him, should be so constant as to be the spring or mover of the rest of the thoughts and actions of our lives.

5. An habitual, intending God as our end, and depending on his support, and subjection to his government, will carry on the soul in a sincere and constant course of godliness, though the actual most observed thoughts of the soul, be fewer in number about God, than about the means that lead unto him, and the occurrences in our way. The soul of man is very active and comprehensive, and can think of several things at once; and when it is once clear and resolved in any case, it can act according to that knowledge and resolution, without any present sensible thought; nay while its actual, most observed thoughts, are upon something else. A musician that hath a habitual skill, can keep time and tune while he is thinking of some other matter. A weaver can cast his shuttle right, and work truly, while he is thinking or talking of other things. A man can eat and drink with discretion, while he talks of other things. Some men can dictate to two or three scribes at once, upon diverse subjects. A traveller can keep on his way, though he seldom think distinctly of his journey's end, but be thinking or discoursing most of the way, upon other matters: for before he undertook his journey he thought both of the end and way, and resolved then which way to go, and that he would go through all both fair and foul, and not turn back till, he saw the place. And this habitual understanding and resolution, may be secretly and unobservedly active, so as to keep a man from erring, and from turning back, though at the same time the traveller's most sensible thoughts and his discourse may be upon something else. When a man is once resolved of his end, and hath laid his design, he is past deliberating of that, and therefore hath less use of his thoughts about it; but is readier to lay them out upon the means, which may be still uncertain, or may require his frequent deliberation. We have usually more thoughts and speeches by the, way, about our company, or our horses, or inns, or other accommodations, or the fairness, or foulness of the way, or other such occurrences, than we have about the place we are going to: and yet this secret intention of our end, will bring us thither. So when a soul hath cast up his accounts, and hath renounced a worldly, sensual felicity, and hath fixed his hopes and resolution upon heaven, and is resolved to cast himself upon Christ, and take God for his only portion, this secret, habitual resolution will do much to keep him constant in the way, though, his thoughts and talk be frequently on other things: yea, when we are thinking of the creature, and feel no actual thoughts of God, it is yet God more than the creature that we think of: for we did beforehand look on the creature as God's work,

representing him unto the world, and as his talents, which we must employ for him, and as every creature is related to him. And this estimation of the creature is still habitually (and in some secret less-perceived act) most prevalent in the soul. Though I am not always sensibly thinking of the king, when I use his coin, or obey his laws, &c. yet it is only as his coin still that I use it, and as his laws that I obey them. Weak habits cannot do their work without great carefulness of thoughts; but perfect habits will act a man with little thoughtfulness, as coming near the natural way of operation. And indeed the imperfection of our habitual godliness doth make our serious thoughts, and vigilancy, and industry to be the more necessary to us.

6. There are some thoughts of God that are necessary to the very being of a holy state; as that God be so much in our thoughts, as to be preferred before all things else, and principally beloved and obeyed; and to the end of our lives, and the bias of our wills. And there are some thoughts of God that are necessary only to the acting and increase of grace.

7. So great is the weakness of our habits, so many and great are the temptations to be overcome, so many difficulties are in our way, and the occasions so various for the exercise of each grace, that it behooveth a Christian to exercise as much thoughtfulness about his end and work, as hath any tendency to promote his work, and to attain his end; but such a thoughtfulness as hindereth us in our work, by stopping, or distracting, or diverting us, is no way pleasing unto God. So excellent is our end, that we can never encourage and delight the mind too much in the forethoughts of it. So sluggish are our hearts, and so loose and unconstant are our apprehensions and resolutions, that we have need to be most frequently quickening them, and lifting at them, and renewing our desires, and suppressing the contrary desires, by the serious thoughts of God and immortality. Our thoughts are the bellows that must kindle the flames of love, desire, hope and zeal. Our thoughts are the spur that must put on a slugglish, tired heart. And so far as they conduce to any such works and ends as these, they are desirable and good. But what master loveth to see his servant sit down and think when he should be at work? Or to use his thoughts only to grieve and vex himself for his faults, but not to mend them. To sit down lamenting that he is so bad and unprofitable a servant, when he should be up and doing his master's business as well as he is able? Such thoughts as hinder us from duty, or discourage, or unfit us for it, are real sins, however they may go under a better name.

8. The godly themselves are very much wanting in the holiness of their thoughts, and the liveliness of their affections. Sense leadeth away the thoughts too easily after these present sensible things; while faith being infirm, the thoughts of God and heaven are much disadvantaged by their invisibility. Many a gracious soul cryeth out, O that I could think as easily, and as affectionately, and as unweariedly about the Lord, and the life to come, as I can do about my friends, my health, my habitation, my business, and other concernments of this life! But, alas, such thoughts of God and heaven, have far more enemies and resistance, than the thoughts of earthly matters have.

9. It is not distracting, vexatious thoughts of God, that the Holy Scriptures call us to; but it is to such thoughts as tend to the healing, and peace, and felicity of the soul; and therefore it is not a melancholy, but a joyful life. If God be better than the world, it must needs be better to think of him. If he be more beloved than any friend, the thoughts of him should be sweeter to us. If he be the everlasting hope and happiness of the soul, it should be a foretaste of happiness to find him

nearest to our hearts. The nature and use of holy thoughts, and of all religion, is but to exalt and sanctify and delight the soul, and bring it up to everlasting rest. And is this the way to melancholy or madness? Or is it not more likely to make men melancholy, to think of nothing but a vain, deceitful and vexatious world, that hath much to disquiet us, but nothing to satisfy us, and can give the soul no hopes of any durable delight?

10. Yet as God is not equally related unto all, so is he not the same to all men's thoughts. If a wicked enemy of God and godliness, be forced and frightened into some thoughts of God, you cannot expect that they should be as sweet and comfortable thoughts, as those of his most obedient children are. While a man is under the guilt and power of his reigning sin, and under the wrath and curse of God, unpardoned, unjustified, a child of the devil, it is not this man's duty to think of God, as if he were fully reconciled to him, and took pleasure in him as in his own. Nor is it any wonder if such a man think of God with fear, and think of his sin with grief and shame. Nor is it any wonder the justified themselves do think of God with fear and grief, when they have provoked him by some sinful and unkind behaviour, or are cast into doubts of their sincerity and interest in Christ, and when he hides his face or assaulteth them with his terrors. To doubt whether a man shall live forever in heaven or hell, may rationally trouble the thoughts of the wisest man in the world; and it were but sottishness not to be troubled at it. David himself could say, "In the day of my trouble I sought the Lord: my sore ran in the night and ceased not: my soul refused to be comforted. I remembered God and was troubled. I complained and my spirit was overwhelmed: thou holdest mine eyes waking. I am so troubled that I cannot speak.—Will the Lord cast off forever?" (Psal. lxxvii. 2-5, 7.)

Yet all the sorrowful thoughts of God, which are the duty either of the godly or the wicked, are but necessary preparatives of their joy. It is not to melancholy, distraction or despair, that God calleth any, even the worst: but it is that the wicked would "Seek the Lord while he may be found, and call upon him while he is near; that he would forsake his way, and the unrighteous man his thoughts; and return unto the Lord, and he will have mercy upon him, and to our God, and he will abundantly pardon." (Isa. lv. 6, 7.) Despair is sin; and the thoughts that tend to it are sinful thoughts, even in the wicked. If worldly crosses, or the sense of danger to the soul had cast any into melancholy, or overwhelmed them with fears, you can name nothing in the world that in reason should be so powerful a remedy to recover them, as the thoughts of God, his goodness, and mercy, and readiness to receive and pardon those that turn unto him, his covenant, and promises, and grace, through Christ, and the everlasting happiness which all may have that will accept and seek it in the time of grace, and prefer it before the deceitful transitory pleasures of the world. If the thoughts of God, and of the heavenly, everlasting joys will not comfort the soul, and cure a sad, despairing mind, I know not what can rationally do it. Though yet it is true, that a presumptuous sinner must needs be in a trembling state, till he find himself at peace with God: and mistaken Christians, that are cast into causeless doubts and fears, by the malice of Satan, are unlikely to walk comfortably with God, till they are resolved and recovered from their mistakes and fears.

CHAPTER V.

Object. But it may be the objector will be ready to think, that 'If it be indeed our duty to walk with God, yet thoughts are no considerable part of it. What more uncertain or mutable than our thoughts? It is deeds and not thoughts that God regardeth. To do no harm to any, but to do good to all, this is indeed to walk with God. You set a man upon a troublesome and impossible work, while you set him upon so strict a guard, and so much exercise of his thoughts. What cares the Almighty for my thoughts?'

Answ. 1. If God knows better than you, and he to be believed, then thoughts are not so inconsiderable as you suppose. Doth he not say, that "the thoughts of the wicked are an abomination to the Lord?" (Prov. xv. 26.) It is the work of the Gospel by its power, to "pull down strongholds, casting down imaginations, and every high thing that exalteth itself against the knowledge of God, and bringing into captivity every thought to the obedience of Christ." (2 Cor. x. 4, 6.) The unrighteous man's forsaking his thoughts, is part of his necessary conversion. (Isa. lv. 7.) It was the description of the deplorate state of the old world, "God saw that the wickedness of man was great in the earth, and that every imagination of the thoughts of his heart, was only evil continually; and it repented the Lord that he had made man on the earth, and it grieved him at his heart." (Gen. vi. 5.) Judge by this, whether thoughts be so little regarded by God, as you imagine. David saith of himself, "I hate vain thoughts." (Psal. cxix. 113.) Solomon saith, "The thoughts of the righteous are right." (Prov. xii. 5.) Paul saith that, "Charity thinketh not evil." (1 Cor. xiii. 5.)

2. Thoughts are the issue of a rational soul. And if its operations be contemptible, its essence is contemptible. If its essence be noble, its operations are considerable. If the soul be more excellent than the body, its operations must be more excellent. To neglect our thoughts and not employ them upon God, and for God, is to vilify our noblest faculties, and deny God, who is a Spirit, that spiritual service which he requireth.

3. Our thoughts are commonly our most cordial, voluntary acts, and show the temper and inclination of the heart: and therefore are regardable to God that searcheth the heart, and calleth first for the service of the heart.

4. Our thoughts are radical and instrumental acts: such as they are, such are the actions of our lives. Christ telleth us that "out of the heart proceed evil thoughts, murders, adulteries, fornications, thefts, false witness, blasphemies, which defile the man." (Matt. xv. 19, 20.)

5. Our thoughts are under a law, as well as words and deeds. "The thought of foolishness is sin." (Prov. xxiv. 9.) And Matt. v. 28, &c. Christ extendeth the law even to the thoughts and desires of the heart. And under the law it is said, "Beware that there be not a thought in thy wicked heart," &c., (Deut. xv. 9.), viz. of unmercifulness towards thy brother.

6. Thoughts can reach higher much than sense, and may be employed upon

45

the most excellent and invisible objects; and therefore are fit instruments to elevate the soul that would converse with God. Though God be infinitely above us, our thoughts may be exercised on him. Our persons never were in heaven, and yet our conversation must be in heaven. (Phil. iii. 20.) And how is that but by our thoughts? Though we see not Christ, yet by the exercise of believing thoughts on him, we love him, and rejoice with joy unspeakable and full of glory. Though God be invisible, yet our "meditations of him may be sweet, and we may delight in the Lord." (Psal. civ. 34.) Say not that all this is but fantastical and delusory, as long as thoughts of things unseen are fitter to actuate and elevate the love, desires and delights of the soul, and to move and guide us in a regular and holy life, than the sense of lesser present good. The thoughts are not vain or delusory, unless the object of them be false and vain,and delusory. Where the object is great, and sure, and excellent, the thoughts of such things are excellent operations of the soul. If the thoughts of vain-glory, wealth and pleasure, can delight the ambitious, covetous and sensual; no wonder if the thoughts of God and life eternal, afford us solid, high delights.

7. The thoughts are not so liable to be counterfeit and hypocritical as are the words and outward deeds: and therefore they show more what the man is, and what is in his heart. For as Solomon saith, "As he thinketh in his heart, so is he." (Prov. xxiii. 7.)

8. Our thoughts may exercise the highest graces of God in man; and also show those graces, as being their effects. How is our faith, and love, and desire, and trust, and joy, and hope to be exercised but by our thoughts? If grace were not necessary and excellent, it would not be wrought by the Spirit of God, and called the Divine Nature, and the Image of God. And if grace be excellent, the use and exercise of it is excellent: and therefore our thoughts by which it is exercised must needs have their excellency too.

9. Our thoughts must be the instruments of our improving all holy truth in Scripture, and all the mercies which we receive, and all the afflictions which we undergo. What good will reading a chapter in the Bible do to anyone that never thinketh on it? "Our delight in the law of God," must engage us to "meditate in it day and night." (Psal. i. 2.) What good shall he get by hearing a sermon that exerciseth not his thoughts for the receiving and digesting it? Our considering what is said, is the way in which we may expect that God should give us "understanding in all things." (2 Tim. ii. 7.) What the better will he be for any of the merciful providences of God, who never bethinks him whence they come, or what is the use and end that they are given for? What good will he get by any afflictions, that never bethinks him, who it is that chastiseth him, and for what, and how he must get them removed, and sanctified to his good. A man is but like one of the pillars in the church, or like the corpse which he treadeth on, or at best but like the dog that followeth him thither for company, if he use not his thoughts about the work which he hath in hand, and cannot say, as Psal. xlviii. 9., "We have thought of thy loving-kindness, O God, in the midst of thy temple." He that biddeth you hear, doth also bid you "Take heed how you hear." (Luke viii. 18.) And you are commanded to "lay up the word in your heart and soul." (Deut. xi. 18, 19.) And to set your hearts to all the words which are testified among you: for it is not a vain thing for you, because it is your life.

10. Our thoughts are so considerable a part of God's service, that they are oft put for the whole. "A book of remembrance was written for them that feared the Lord, and that thought upon his name." (Mal. iii. 16.) Our believing and loving

God, and trusting in him, and desiring him and his grace, are the principal parts of his service, which are exercised immediately by our thoughts: and in praise and prayer it is this inward part that is the soul and life of all. He is a foolish hypocrite that thinks "to be heard for his much speaking." (Matt. vi. 7.)

And on the contrary, the thoughts are named as the sum of all iniquity. "Their thoughts are thoughts of iniquity." (Isa. lxix. 7.) "I have spread out my hands all the day long unto a rebellious people, which walketh in a way that was not good, after their own thoughts." (Isa. lxv. 2.) "O Jerusalem, wash thy heart from wickedness that thou mayest be saved: how long shall thy vain thoughts lodge within thee! (Jer. iv. 14.) "The fool hath said in his heart there is no God." (Psal. xiv. 1.)

11. A man's thoughts are the appointed orderly way for the conversion of a sinner, and the preventing of his sin and misery. David saith, "I thought on my ways, and turned my feet unto thy testimonies." (Psal. cxix. 69.) The prodigal "came to himself," and returned to his father, by the success of his own consideration. (Luke xv. 17, 18.) "Thus saith the Lord of Hosts, Consider your ways," (Hag. i. 5.), is a voice that every sinner should hear. "It is he that considereth and doth not according to his father's sins, that shall not die." (Ezek. xviii. 14.) Therefore it is God's desire, "O that they were wise and understood this, and that they would consider their latter end." (Deut. xxxii. 29.) It is either men's inconsiderateness, or the error of their thoughts, that is the cause of all their wickedness. "My people doth not consider." (Isa. i. 3.) Paul "verily thought that he ought to do many things against the name of Jesus." (Acts xxvi. 9.) Many "deceive themselves by thinking themselves something when they are nothing." (Gal. vi. 3.) "They think it strange that we run not with them to excess of riot:" and therefore "they speak evil of us." (1 Pet. iv. 4.) Disobedient formalists "consider not that they do evil," when they think that they are offering acceptable sacrifices to God. (Eccles. v. 1, 2.) The very murder of God's holy ones hath proceeded from these erroneous thoughts; "They that kill you shall think they do God service." (John xvi. 2.) All the ambition, and covetousness, and injustice and cruelty following thereupon, which troubleth the world, and ruineth men's souls, is from their erroneous thoughts, overvaluing these deceitful things. "Their inward thought is that their houses shall continue forever, and their dwelling places to all generations." (Psal. xlix. 11.) The presumptuous and impenitent are surprised by destruction, for want of thinking of it to prevent it: "In such an hour as you think not, the Son of man cometh."

12. Lastly, The thoughts are the most constant actions of a man, and therefore most of the man is in them. We are not always reading, or hearing, or praying, or working: but we are always thinking. And therefore it doth especially concern us to see that this constant breath of the soul be sweet, and that this constant stream be pure and run in the right channel. Well therefore did David make this his request; "Search me, O God, and know my heart: try me, and know my thoughts; and see if there be any wicked way in me, and lead me in the way everlasting." (Psal. cxxxix. 23, 24.) I say therefore to those that insist on this irrational objection, that these very thoughts of theirs, concerning the inconsiderableness of thoughts, are so foolish and ungodly, that when they understand the evil even of these, they will know that thoughts were more to be regarded. "If therefore thou hast done foolishly in lifting up thyself, or if thou hast thought evil, lay thy hand upon thy mouth."

And though after all this, I still confess that it is so exceeding hard a matter to keep the thoughts in holy exercise and order, that even the best do daily and hourly sin, in the omissions, the disorder or vanity of their thoughts; yet for all that, we must needs conclude that the inclination and design of our thoughts must be principally for God, and that the thoughts are principal instruments of the soul, in acting it in his service, and moving it towards him, and in all this holy work of our walking with God: and therefore to imagine that thoughts are inconsiderable and of little use, is to unman us, and unchristen us. The labour of the mind is necessary for the attaining the felicity of the mind; as the labour of the body is necessary for the things that belong unto the body. As bodily idleness bringeth unto beggary, when the diligent hand makes rich; so the idleness of the soul doth impoverish the soul, when the laborious Christian liveth plentifully and comfortably through the blessing of God upon his industry and labour. You cannot expect that God should appear to you in a bodily shape, that you may have immediate converse with him in the body. The corporal eating of him in transubstantiated bread, supposed common to men, and mice, or dogs, we leave to Papists, who have made themselves a singular new religion, in despite of the common sense and reason of mankind, as well as of the Scriptures and the judgment of the church. It is in the Spirit that thou must converse with God who is a Spirit. The mind seeth him by faith, who is invisible to the bodily eyes. Nay, if you will have a true and saving knowledge of God, you must not liken him to anything that is visible, nor have any corporal conceivings of him. Earthly things may be the glass in which we may behold him, while we are here in the flesh; but our conceivings of him must be spiritual, and minds that are immersed in flesh and earth, are unmeet to hold communion with him. The natural man knoweth him not, and the "carnal mind is enmity to him, and they that are in the flesh cannot please him." (Rom. viii.) It is the pure, abstracted, elevated soul, that understandeth by experience what it is to walk with God.

CHAPTER VI.

§ 1. Having in the foregoing uses, reproved the atheism and contempt of God, which ungodly men are continually guilty of, and endeavoured to convince them of the necessity and desirableness of walking with God, and in particular of improving our thoughts for holy converse with him, and answered the objections of the impious and atheists; I shall next endeavour to cure the remnants of this disease in those that are sincerely holy, who live too strangely to God their Father in the world. In the performance of this, I shall first show you what are the benefits of this holy life, which should make it appear desirable and delightful. 2. I shall show you why believers should addict themselves to it as doubly obliged, and that their neglect of it is a sin attended with special aggravations. This is the remainder of my task.

§ 2. I. To walk with God in a holy and heavenly conversation, is the employment most suitable to human nature, not to its corrupt disposition, nor to the carnal interest and appetite; but to nature as nature, to man as man. It is the very work that he was made for: the faculties and frame of the soul and body were composed for it by the wise Creator: they are restored for it by the gracious Redeemer. Though in corrupted nature, where sensuality is predominant, there is an estrangedness from God, and an enmity and hatred of him, so that the wicked are more averse to all serious, holy converse with him (in prayer, contemplation, and a heavenly life) than they are to a worldly sinful life; yet all this is but the disease of nature, corrupting its appetite, and turning it against that proper food, which is most suitable to its sound desires, and necessary to its health and happiness. Though sinful habits are become as it were a second nature to the ungodly, so depraving their judgments and desires, that they verily think the business and pleasures of the flesh are most suitable to them; yet these are as contrary to nature as nature, that is, to the primitive tendencies of all our faculties, and the proper use to which they were fitted by our Creator, and to that true felicity which is the end of all our parts and powers, even as madness is contrary to the rational nature, though it were hereditary.

1. What can be more agreeable to the nature of man, than to be rational and wise, and to live in the purest exercise of reason? And certainly there is nothing more rational than that we should live to God, and gladly accept of all that communion with him which our natures on earth are capable of. Nothing can be more reasonable than for the reasonable soul to be entirely addicted to him that did create it, that doth preserve it, and by whom it doth subsist and act. Nothing is more reasonable than that the absolute Lord of nature be honoured and served wholly by his own. Nothing is more reasonable than that the reasonable creature do live in the truest dependence upon, and subordination to the highest reason; and that derived, imperfect, defectible wisdom, be subservient to, and guided by the primitive, perfect, indefectible wisdom. It is most reasonable that the children depend upon the Father, and the foolish be ruled by the most wise, and that the

49

subjects be governed by the universal King; and that they honour him and obey him, and that the indigent apply themselves to him that is all sufficient, and is most able and ready to supply their wants; and that the impotent rest upon him that is Omnipotent.

2. Nothing can be more reasonable, than that the reasonable nature should intend its end, and seek after its true and chief felicity: and that it should love good as good, and therefore prefer the chiefest good before that which is transitory and insufficient. Reason commandeth the reasonable creature to avoid its own delusion and destruction, and to rest upon him that can everlastingly support us, and not upon the creature that will deceive us and undo us: and to prefer the highest and noblest converse before that which is inferior, unprofitable, and base, and that we rejoice more in the highest, purest, and most durable delights, than in those that are sordid, and of short continuance. And who knoweth not that God is the chiefest good, and true felicity of man, the everlasting rock, the durable delight, and to be preferred before his creatures? And who might not find, that would use his reason, that all things below are vanity and vexation?

3. Nothing can be more rational and agreeable to man's nature, than that the superior faculties should govern the inferior, that the brutish part be subject to the rational; and that the ends and objects of this higher faculty be preferred before the objects of the lower; that the objects of sense be made subservient to the objects of reason. If this be not natural and rational, then it is natural to man to be no man, but a beast, and reasonable to be unreasonable. Now it is evident that a holy living unto God, is but the improvement of true reason, and its employment for and upon its noblest object, and its ultimate end: and that a sensual life is the exercise of the inferior, brutish faculties, in predominancy above and before the rational: and therefore to question whether God or the creature should be first sought, and loved, and principally desired, and delighted in, and served, is but to question whether we should live like men or like beasts, and whether dogs or wise men be the fitter companions for us? And whether the rider or the horse should have the rule? Whether the rational or sensitive powers be superior and proper to the nature of a man?

Object. 'But there is a middle state of life betwixt the sensual and the divine or holy life, which sober philosophers did live, and this is the most natural life, and most properly so called.'

Answ. I deny this. There is no middle state of life, if you denominate the several states of life, from the several ends, or the several powers. I grant that the very sensitive powers in man, especially the imagination, is much advanced by the conjunction of reason, above that of a brute: and I grant that the delights of the phantasy may be preferred before the immediate pleasure of the senses: and I grant that some little distant knowledge of God, and things divine, and hopes of attaining them, may affect an unsanctified man with an answerable pleasure. But all this is nothing to prove that there is a third sort of end, or of powers, and so a third or middle state of life, specifically distinct from the sensitive and the holy life. Besides, the vegetative man hath no other life or faculties, than the sensitive and the rational: and therefore one of these must be in predominancy or rule. And therefore he can have no middle sort or end; and therefore no middle state of life, that can be said to be agreeable to his nature. Those that seek and take up their chief felicity in riches and plenty, and provisions for the flesh, though not in present pleasing of the sense, do live but the life of sensuality. A fox or dog takes pleasure when he hath eaten his belly full, to hide and lay up the rest: and so doth the bee to fill the hive, and make provision for the winter. The proud that delight in honour and applause, and making others subject to their lusts, do live but the life of sensuality: a dog, a horse, and other brutes, have something of the same. They that are grave through melancholy, or because they can reach no great matter in the world, and because their old or duller spirits are not much pleased with juvenile delights, and so live retiredly, and seek no higher pleasure or felicity, but only sit down with the weeping or the laughing philosopher, lamenting or deriding the vanity of the world, do yet live no other than a sensual life: as an old dog that hath no pleasure in hunting or playfulness, as he had when he was a whelp. Only he is less deluded, and less vain, than other sensualists that find more pleasure in their course.

All the doubt is concerning those that place their felicity in knowledge, and those that delight in moral virtues, or that delight in studying of God, though they are no Christians.

Answ. The point is weighty, and hath oft unhappily fallen into injudicious hands. I shall endeavour to resolve it as truly, clearly, and impartially as I can. 1. It is a great error against the nature of man, to say, that knowledge as such, is fit to be any man's chief and ultimate end. It may be that act which is next the enjoying act of the will, which is it that indeed is next the end, objectively considered: but it is not that act which we call 'ultimate ultimus.' And this is plain, 1. Because the object of the understanding, which is truth, is not formally the nearest object or matter of full felicity or delight: it is goodness that is the nearest object. 2. And therefore the office of the intellect is but introductive and subservient to the office of the will, to apprehend the verity of good, and present it to the will to be prosecuted or embraced, or delighted in. There are many truths that are ungrateful and vexatious, and which men would wish to be no truths. And there is a knowledge which is troublesome, useless, undesirable and tormenting, which even a wise man would fain avoid, if he knew how. Morality is but preparatively in the intellect: and therefore intellectual acts, as such, are not morally good, or evil, but only participatively, as subject to the will. And therefore knowledge, as such, being not a moral good, can be no other than such a natural good as is 'bonum alicui,' only so far as it tendeth to some welfare or happiness, or pleasure of the possessor or some other: and this welfare or pleasure is either that which is suited to the sensitive powers, or to the rational (which is to be found in the love of God alone).

2. I add therefore, that even those men that seem to take up their felicity in common knowledge, indeed do but make their knowledge subservient to something else which they take for their felicity. For knowledge of evil may torment them. It is only to know something which they take to be good, that is their delight. And it is the complacency or love of that good at the heart, which sets them on work, and causeth the delight of knowing. If you will say that common knowledge, as knowledge, doth immediately delight, yet will it be found but such a pleasing of the phantasy, as an ape hath in spying marvels, which if it have no end that is higher, is still but a sensitive delight; but if it be referred to a higher delight (in God) it doth participate of the nature of it. Delight in general is the common end of men and brutes: but in specie they are distinguished as sensual or rational.

3. If you suppose a philosopher to be delighted in studying mathematics, or any of the works of God, either he hath herein an end, or no end beyond the knowledge of the creature: either he terminateth his desires and delights in the creature, or else useth it as a means to raise him to the Creator. If he study and delight in the creature ultimately, this is indeed the act of a rational creature, and

an act of reason, as to the faculty it proceeds from (and so is a rational contrivance for sensual ends and pleasures): but it is but the error of reason, and is no more agreeable to the rational nature, than the deceit; of the senses is to the sensitive. Nor is it finally to be numbered with the operations felicitating human nature, any more than an erroneous dream of pleasure, or than that man is to be numbered with the lovers of learning, who taketh pleasure in the binding, leaves, or letters of the book, while he understandeth nothing of the sense. But if this philosopher seek to know the Creator in and by the creatures, and take delight in the Maker's power, wisdom and goodness, which appeareth in them, then this is truly a rational delight, in itself considered, and beseeming a man. And if he reach so far in it, as to make God his highest desire and delight, overpowering the desires and delights of sensuality, he shall be happy, as being led by the Son unto the Father: but if he make but some little approaches towards it, and drown all such desires in the sensual desires and delights, he is then but an unhappy sensualist, and liveth brutishly in the tenor of his life, though in some acts in part he operate rationally as a man.

The like I may say of them that are said to place their delight in moral virtues. Indeed, nothing is properly a moral good (or virtue) but that which is exercised upon God as our end, or upon the creature as a means to this end. To study and know mere notions of God, or what is to be held and said of him in discourse, is not to study to know God, no more than to love the language and phrase of holy writing, is to love God. To study God, as one that is less regardable and desirable than our sensual delights, is but to blaspheme him. To study, seek and serve him as one that can promote or hinder our sensual felicity, is but to abuse him as a means to your sensuality. And for the virtues of temperance, justice, or charity, they are but analogically and 'secundum quid' to be found in any ungodly person. Materially they may have them in an eminent degree; but not as they are informed by the end which moralizeth them. Jezebel's fast was not formally a virtue, but an odious way of hypocrisy to oppress the innocent. He that doth works of justice and mercy, to evil ends only (as for applause, or to deceive, &c.) and not from the true principles of justice and mercy, doth not thereby exercise moral virtue, but hypocrisy, and other vice. He that doth works of justice and mercy, out of mere natural compassion to others, and desire of their good, without respect to God, as obliging, or rewarding, or desiring it, doth perform such a natural good work, as a lamb or a gentle beast doth to his fellows, which hath not the true form of moral virtue, but the matter only. He that in such works hath some little by-respect to God, but more to his carnal interest among men, doth that which on the by, participateth of moral good, or is such 'secundum quid,' but not 'simpliciter,' being to be denominated from the part predominant. He that doth works of justice or charity principally to please God, and in true obedience to his will, and a desire to be conformed thereto, doth that which is formally a moral good, and holy, though there may be abhorred mixtures of worse respects.

So that there are but two states of life here: one of those that walk after the flesh, and the other of those that walk after the Spirit. However the flesh hath several materials and ways of pleasure: and even the rational actings that have a carnal end, are carnal finally and morally, though they are acts of reason; for they are but the errors of reason, and defectiveness of true rationality; and being but the acts of erroneous reason as captivated by the flesh, and subservient to the carnal interest, they are themselves to be denominated carnal: and so even the reasonable soul as biased by sensuality, and captivated thereto, is included in the name of 'flesh' in the Scripture.

How much moral good is in that course of piety or obedience to God, which proceedeth only from the fear of God's judgments, without any love to him; I shall not now discuss, because I have too far digressed already.

All that I have last said, is to show you the reasonableness of living unto God, as being indeed the proper and just employment of the superior faculties of the soul, and the government of the lower faculties. For if any other, called moralists, do seem to subject the sensual life to the rational, either they do but seem to do so; the sensual interest being indeed predominant, and their rational operations subjected thereto: or at the best, it is but some poor and erroneous employment of the rational faculties which they exercise, or some weak approaches towards that high and holy life, which is indeed the life which the rational nature was created for; and which is the right improvement of it.

4. Moreover, nothing is more beseeming the nature of man, than to aspire after the highest and noblest improvement of itself; and to live the most excellent life that it is capable of. For every nature tendeth to its own perfection. But it is most evident, that to walk with God in holiness, is a thing that human nature is capable of; and that is the highest life that we are capable of on earth: and therefore it is the life most suitable to our natures.

5. And what can be more rational and beseeming a created nature, than to live to those ends, which our Creator intended in the very forming of our natures? It is his ends that are principally to be served. But the very composure of our faculties plainly prove, that his end was that we should be tilted for his service: he gave us no powers or capacity in vain: and therefore to serve him and walk with him, is most suitable to our natures.

Object. 'That is natural which is first, and born with us: but our enmity to holiness is first, and not our holiness.'

Answ. It may be called natural indeed, because it is first, and born with us: and in that respect we confess that sin, and not holiness, is natural to us. But holiness is called natural to us, in a higher respect, because it was the primitive, natural constitution of man, and was before sin, and is the perfection or health of nature, and the right employment and improvement of it, and tends to its happiness. An hereditary leprosy may be called natural, it is first, and before health in that person: but health and soundness is natural, as being the well-being of nature, when the leprosy is unnatural, as being but its disease, and tending to its destruction.

Object. 'But nature in its first constitution was not holy, but innocent only, and it was by a superadded gift of grace that it became holy, as some schoolmen think, and as others think, Adam had no holiness till his restoration.'

Answ. These are Popish improved fancies, and contrary to nature and the word of God. 1. They are nowhere written, nor have any evidence in nature, and therefore are the groundless dreams of men.

2. The work of our recovery to God is called in Scripture a redemption, renovation, restoration, which imply that nature was once in that holy estate before the fall. And it is expressly said, that the "new man" which we "put on, is renewed in knowledge after the image of him that created him." (Col. iii. 10.) And after God's image Adam was created.

3. If it belong to the soundness and integrity of nature to be holy, (that is, disposed and addicted to live to God) then it is rash and foolish for men out of their own imagination, to feign that God first made nature defective, and then mended it by superadded grace. But if it belong not to the soundness and integrity of hu-

man nature to be holy, then why did God give him grace to make him so? Nay, then it would follow, that when God sanctified Adam, or any since, he made him specifically another thing, another creature, of another nature, and did not only cure the diseases of his nature.

4. It is yet apparent in the very nature of man's faculties, that their very usefulness and tendency, is to live to God, and to enjoy him: and that God should make a nature apt for such a use, and give it no disposedness to its proper use, is an unnatural conceit. We see to this day that it is but an unreasonable abuse of reason, when it is not used holily for God; and it is a very disease of nature to be otherwise disposed. Therefore primitive nature had such a holy inclination.

5. The contrary opinion tendeth to infidelity, and to brutify human nature. For if no man can believe that he must be holy, and live to God, and enjoy him hereafter in heaven, but he that also believeth that primitive nature was never disposed or qualified for such a life; and that God must first make a man another creature in specie, of another nature (and consequently not a man) this is not only improbable, but so contrary to Scripture and reason, that few considerate persons would believe it. As if we must believe that God would turn brutes into men. God healeth, elevateth, and perfecteth nature, but doth not specifically change it, at least in this life.

Object. 'But let it be granted that he giveth no man specifically another nature, yet he may give him such higher gifts, as may be like another nature to him so far.'

Answ. No doubt he may and doth give him such gifts as actuate and perfect nature: but some disposition to our ultimate end is essential to our nature; and therefore to assign man another ultimate end, and to give a disposition to it, of which he had no seed, or part, or principle before, is to make him another creature. I confess that in lapsed man, the holy disposition is so far dead, as that the change maketh a man a new creature in a moral sense (as he is a new man that changeth his mind and manners): but still nature hath its aptitude, as rational, to be employed for its Maker; so that he is not a new creature in a natural sense.

An actual or habitual willingness to his holy employment, a promptitude to it, and a due understanding of it, is the new creature, morally so called, which is given in our sanctification: but the natural aptitude that is in our faculties as rational, to this holy life, is essential to us as men, or as rational; even to have the 'potentiam naturalem' which must yet have further help or moral life to actuate it. And Adam had both these: the one he retained, or else he had not continued a man; the other he lost, or else he had not had need of renovation.

6. If Adam's nature had not been disposed to God, as to his end and sovereign, then the law of nature (to adhere to God, and obey and serve him) was not written in his heart: and then it would not have been his duty to adhere to God, and to obey and serve him; which is so false, that even in lapsed, unrenewed nature, there is left so much aptitude hereto, as will prove him to be still under the obligations of this law of nature, even actually to adhere to God, and to obey him, which a dead man, a mad man, or an infant, is not (immediately).

By all this you see, that though the blindness and disease of reason, is contrary to faith and holiness, yet reason itself is so much for it, as that faith itself is but the act of elevated well informed reason; and supernatural revelation is but the means to inform our reason, about things which have not a natural evidence, discernable by us. And sanctification (actively taken) is but the healing of our reason and rational appetite: and holiness is but the health or soundness of them.

The error of reason must be renounced by believers; but not the use of reason: the sufficiency of reason and natural light, without supernatural light and help, we must all deny: but to set reason, as reason, in opposition to faith or holiness, or divine revelation, is as gross a piece of foolery, as to set the visive faculty in opposition to the light of the sun, or to its objects. It is the unreasonableness of sinners that is to be cured by illuminating grace. "They are wise to do evil, but to do good they have no knowledge." Their reason is wounded, depraved and corrupted about the matters of God: they have reason to serve the flesh, but not to master it. God doth renew men by giving them wisdom, and bringing them to a sound mind: as logic helpeth reason in discourse and arguing, so theology informeth reason about the matters of God and our salvation: and the Spirit of God doth make his doctrine and revelation effectual. Make nature sound, and reason clear, and then we will consent that all men be persuaded to live according to their nature and their reason. But if a bedlam will rave and tear himself and others, and say, This is according to my nature or my reason; it is fitter that chains and whips do cure that nature and reason, than that he be allowed to live according to his madness. If a drunkard or whoremonger will say, My nature and reason incline me to please my appetite and lust, it is fit that the swinish nature be corrected, and the beast which rideth and ruleth the man, be taken down; and when indeed his nature is the nature of man, and fitted to the use and ends it was made for, then let him live according to it and spare not. If a malicious man will abuse or kill his neighbour, and say, This is according to my nature, let that nature be used as the nature of wolves and foxes, and other noxious creatures are. But let human nature be cured of its blindness, carnality, and corruption, and then it will need no external testimony to convince it, that no employment is so natural and suitable to man, as to walk with God, in love and confidence, and reverent worship, and cheerful obedience to his will. A worldly, fleshly, sensual life, will then appear to be below the rational nature of a man, as it is below us to go to grass with horses, or to live as mere companions of brutes. It will then appear to be as natural for us to love and live to our Creator and Redeemer, and to walk with God, as for a child to love his parents, and to live with them and serve them. When I say that this is natural, I mean not that it is necessary by natural necessity, or that grace doth operate 'per modum naturae,' as their rational motion is so called. There is a brutish or inanimate nature, and there is a rational, voluntary nature. Grace worketh not according to the way of inanimate nature, in free agents. I may well say, that whatever is rational, is natural to a rational creature as such, so far as he discerneth it. Yea, and habits, though they effect not necessarily, but freely in a rational nature, yet they incline necessarily, 'et per modum naturae.' They contain in their being a natural aptitude and propensity to action.

Object. 'But thus you confound nature and grace, natural and supernatural operations, while you make grace natural'.

Answ. No such matter. Though walking with God be called natural, as it is most agreeable to nature so far as it is sound, and is the felicity and meetest employment of the rational nature as such: yet, 1. Diseased nature doth abhor it, as a diseased stomach the pleasantest and most wholesome food, (as I said before). 2. And this disease of nature cannot be cured without divine, supernatural grace. So that as to the efficient cause, our holiness is supernatural. But it is unsound doctrine of those that affirm that Adam in his pure, natural state of innocence, had no natural holiness, or aptitude and promptitude to walk with God in order to everlasting happiness; but say that all this was either wanting to him, and was a state specifically distinct, which he fell short of by his sin, or that it was given him by superadded grace, and was not in his entire nature.

And yet we deny not but as to degrees, Adam's nature was to grow up to more perfection: and that his natural holiness contained not a sufficient immediate aptitude and promptitude to every duty which might afterward be required of him; but this was to be obtained in the exercise of that holiness which he had: even as a vine or other fruit tree, though it be natural to it to bear its proper fruit, yet hath it not an immediate sufficient aptitude hereto, whilst it is but appearing out of the seed, before it be grown up to just maturity. Or as it is natural to a man to discourse and reason; but yet his nature in infancy, or untaught and unexercised, hath not a sufficient immediate aptitude and promptitude hereunto. Or as grace inclineth a renewed soul to every holy truth and duty; and yet such a soul in its infancy of grace, hath not a sufficient, immediate aptitude or promptitude to the receiving of every holy truth, or the doing of every holy duty; but must grow up to it by degrees. But the addition of these degrees, is no specifical alteration of the nature of man, or of that grace which was before received.

Having been so long upon this first consideration (that walking with God is most agreeable to human nature) I shall be more brief in the rest that follow.

II. To walk with God, and live to him, is incomparably the highest and noblest life. To converse with men only, is to converse with worms: whether they be princes or poor men, they differ but as the bigger vermin from the lesser. If they be wise and good, their converse may be profitable and delightful, because they have a beam of excellency from the face of God: (And O how unspeakable is the distance between his wisdom and goodness, and theirs!) But if they be foolish, ungodly and dishonest, how loathsome is their conversation! What stinking breath is in their profane and filthy language, in their lives and slanders of the just, in their sottish jeers and scorns of those that walk with God which expose at once their folly and misery to the pity of all that are truly understanding. When they are gravely speaking evil of the things which they understand not, or with a fleering confidence deriding merrily the holy commands and ways of God, they are much more lamentably expressing their infatuation, than any that are kept in chains in bedlam: though indeed, with the most, they escape the reputation which they deserve, because they are attended with persons of their own proportion of wisdom, that always reverence a silken coat, and judge them wise that wear gold lace, and have the greatest satisfaction of their wills and lusts, and are able to do most mischief in the world: and because good man have learned to honour the worst of their superiors, and not to call them as they are. But God is bold to call them as they are, and give them in his word, such names and characters by which they might come to know themselves. And is it not a higher, nobler life to walk with God, than to converse in bedlam, or with intoxicated sensualists, that live in a constant deliration.

Yea, worse than so: ungodly men are "children of the devil," so called by Jesus Christ himself, (John viii. 44.), because they have much of the nature of the devil, and the lusts of their father they will do; yea, they "are taken captive by him at his will." (2 Tim. ii. 26.) They are "the servants of sin," and do the drudgery that so vile a master sets them on. (John viii. 34.) Certainly as the spirits of the just are so like to angels, that Christ saith, we shall be as they, and equal to them; so the wicked are nearer kin to devils, than they themselves will easily believe. They are as like him as children to their father. He is a liar, and so are they. He is a hater of God, and godliness, and godly men, and so are they. He is a murderer, and would fain devour the holy seed; and such are they. He envieth the progress of the Gospel, and the prosperity of the church, and the increase of holiness, and so do they. He hath a special malice against the most powerful and successful preachers of the word of God, and against the most zealous and eminent saints; and so have they. He cares not by what lies and fictions he disgraceth them, nor how cruelly he useth them; no more do they, (or some of them at least). He cherisheth licentiousness, sensuality and impiety; and so do they. If they do seem better in their adversity and restraint, yet try them but with prosperity, and power, and you shall see quickly how like they are to devils. And shall we delight more to converse with brutes and incarnate devils, than with God? Is it not a more high and excellent conversation to walk with God, and live to him, than to be companions of such degenerate men, that have almost forfeited the reputation of humanity? Alas! they are companions so deluded and ignorant, and yet so willful; so miserable, and yet so confident and secure, that they are, to a believing eye, the most lamentable sight that the whole world can show us out of hell. And how sad a life must it then needs be, to converse with such, were it not for the hope that we have of furthering their recovery and salvation!

But to walk with God is a word so high, that I should have feared the guilt of arrogance in using it, if I had not found it in the holy Scriptures. It is a word that importeth so high and holy a frame of soul, and expresseth such high and holy actions, that the naming of it striketh my heart with reverence, as if I had heard the voice to Moses, "Put off thy shoes from off thy feet, for the place whereon thou standeth is holy ground." (Exod. iii. 5.) Methinks he that shall say to me, Come see a man that walks with God, doth call me to see one that is next unto an angel, or glorified soul! It is a far more reverend object in mine eye, than ten thousand lords or princes, considered only in their fleshly glory. It is a wiser action for people to run and crowd together, to see a man that walks with God, than to see the pompous train of princes, their entertainments, or their triumph. O happy man, that walks with God, though neglected and contemned by all about him! What blessed sights doth he daily see! What ravishing tidings, what pleasant melody doth he daily hear, unless it be in his swoons or sickness! What delectable food doth he daily taste! He seeth by faith the God, the glory, which the blessed spirits see at hand by nearest intuition! He seeth that in a glass and darkly, which they behold with open face! He seeth the glorious Majesty of his Creator, the eternal King, the Cause of causes, the Composer, Upholder, Preserver, and Governor of all the worlds! He beholdeth the wonderful methods of his providence: and what he cannot reach to see, he admireth, and waiteth for the time when that also shall be open to his view! He seeth by faith the world of spirits, the hosts that attend the throne of God; their perfect righteousness, their full devotedness to God; their ardent love, their flaming zeal, their ready and cheerful obedience, their dignity and shining glory, in which the lowest of them exceedeth that which the disciples saw on Moses and Elias when they appeared on the holy mount, and talked with Christ! They hear by faith the heavenly concert, the high and harmonious songs of praise, the joyful triumphs of crowned saints, the sweet commemorations of the things that were done and suffered on earth, with the praises of him that redeemed them by his blood, and made them kings and priests to God: herein he hath sometimes a sweet foretaste of the everlasting pleasures, which though it be but little, as Jonathan's honey on the end of his rod, or as the clusters of grapes which were brought from Canaan into the wilderness, yet are they more excellent than all the delights of sinners· And in the beholding of this celestial glory, some beams do penetrate his breast, and so irradiate his longing soul, that he is changed thereby into the same image, from glory to glory; the Spirit of Glory and of God doth rest upon him. And O what an excellent holy frame doth this converse with God possess his soul of! How reverently doth he think of him! What life is there in every name and attribute of God which he heareth or thinketh on! The mention of his power, his wisdom, his goodness, his love, his holiness, his truth, how powerful and how pleasant are they to him when to those that know him but by the hearing of the ear, all these are but like common names and notions; and even to the weaker sort of Christians, whose walking with God is more uneven, and low, interrupted by their sins, and doubts, and fears, this life and glory of a Christian course, is less perceived.

And the sweet appropriating and applying works of faith, by which the soul can own his God, and finds himself owned by him, are exercised most easily and happily in these near approaches unto God. Our doubts are cherished by our darkness, and that is much caused by our distance: the nearer the soul doth approach to God, the more distinctly it heareth the voice of mercy, the sweet reconciling invitations of love; and the more clearly it discerneth that goodness and amiableness in God, which maketh it easier to us to believe that he loveth us, or is ready to embrace us; and banisheth all those false and horrid apprehensions of him, which before were our discouragement, and made him seem to us more terrible than amiable. As the ministers and faithful servants of Christ, are ordinarily so misrepresented by the malignant devil, to those that know them not, that they are ready to think them some silly fools, or false-hearted hypocrites, and to shun them as strange undesirable persons; but when they come to thorough acquaintance with them by a nearer and familiar converse, they see how much they were mistaken, and wronged by their prejudice and belief of slanderers' misreports: even so a weak believer, that is under troubles, in the apprehension of his sin and danger, is apt to hearken to the enemy of God, that would show him nothing but his wrath, and represent God as an enemy to him: and in this case it is exceeding hard for a poor sinner to believe that God is reconciled to him, or loveth him, or intends him good, but he is ready to dread and shun him as an enemy, or as he would fly from a wild beast or murderer, or from fire or water, that would destroy him: and all these injurious thoughts of God are cherished by strangeness and disacquaintance. But as the soul doth fall into an understanding and serious converse with God, and having been often with him, doth find him more merciful than he was by Satan represented to him, his experience reconcileth his mind to God, and maketh it much easier to him to believe that God is reconciled unto him, when he hath found much better entertainment with God than he expected, and hath observed his benignity, and the treasures of his bounty laid up in Christ, and by him distributed to believers, and hath found him ready to hear and help, and found him the only full and suitable felicitating good, this banisheth his former horrid thoughts, and maketh him ashamed that ever he should think so suspiciously, injuriously, and dishonourably of his dearest God and Father.

Yet I must confess that there are many upright, troubled souls, that are much in reading, prayer, and meditation, that still find it hard to be persuaded of the love of God, and that have much more disquietment and fear since they set themselves to think of God, than they had before. But yet for all this, we may well conclude, that to walk with God, is the way to consolation, and tendeth to acquaint us with his love. As for those troubled souls, whose experience is objected against this, some of them are such as are yet but in their return to God, from a life of former sin and misery, and are yet but like the needle in the compass that is shaken, in a trembling motion towards their rest, and not in any settled apprehensions of it. Some of them by the straying of their imaginations too high, and putting themselves upon more than their heads can bear, and by the violence of fears, or other passions, do make themselves incapable of those sweet consolations which else they might find in their converse with God; as a lute, when the strings are broken with straining, is incapable of making any melody. All of them have false apprehensions of God, and therefore trouble themselves by their own mistakes. And if some perplex themselves by their error, doth it follow that therefore the truth is not comfortable? Is not a father's presence consolatory, because some children are afraid of their fathers, that know them not because of some disguise? And some of God's children walk so unevenly and carelessly before him, that their sins provoke him to hide his face, and to seem to reject them and disown them, and so to trouble them that he may bring them home: but shall the comforts of our Father's love and family be judged of by the fears or smart of those whom he is scourging for their disobedience, or their trial? Seek God with understanding, as knowing his essential properties, and what he will be to them that sincerely and diligently seek him; and then you will quickly have experience, that nothing so much tendeth to quiet and settle a doubting, troubled, unstable soul, as faithfully to walk with God.

But the soul that estrangeth itself from God, may indeed for a time have the quietness of security; but (so far) it will be strange to the assurance of his love, and to true consolation. Expect not that God should follow you with his comforts in your sinfulness and negligence, and cast them into your hearts whilst you neither seek nor mind them; or that he will give you the fruit of his ways in your own ways. Will he be your joy when you forget him? Will he delight your souls with his goodness and amiableness, while you are taken up with other matters, and think not of him? Can you expect to find the comforts of his family, among his enemies, out of doors? The experience of all the world can tell you, that prodigals, while they are straggling from their Father's house, do never taste the comforts of his embraces; the strangers meddle not with his children's joys: they grow not in the way of ambition, covetousness, vainglory, or sensuality; but in the way of holy obedience, and of believing contemplations of the divine, everlasting objects of delight. "For, lo, they that are far from him shall perish. He destroyeth them that go a whoring from him. But it is good for us to draw nigh to God." (Psal. lxxiii. 27,28.)

III. Walking with God is the only course that can prove and make men truly wise. It proves them wise that make so wise and good a choice, and are disposed and skilled in any measure for so high a work. Practical wisdom is the solid, useful, profitable wisdom: and practical wisdom is seen in our choice of good, and refusal of evil, as its most immediate and excellent effect. And no choosing or refusing doth show the wisdom or folly of man so much as that which is about the greatest matters, and which everlasting life or death depend on. He is not thought so wise among men that can write a volume about the orthography or etymology of a word, or can guess what wood the Trojan horse was made of, or that can make a chain to tie a flea in, as he that can bring home gold and pearls, or he that can obtain and manage governments, or he that can cure mortal maladies. For as in lading we difference bulk and value, and take not that for the best commodity which is of greatest quantity or weight, but that which is most precious and of greatest use; so there is a bulky knowledge, extended far, to a multitude of words and things, which are all of no great use or value; and therefore the knowledge of them is such as they: and there is a precious sort of knowledge, which fixeth upon the most precious things; which being of greatest use and value, do accordingly prove the knowledge such. Nothing will prove a man simply and properly wise, but that which will prove or make him happy. He is wise indeed, that is wise to his own and others' good; and that is indeed his good, which saveth his soul, and maketh him forever blessed. Though we may admire the cunning of those that can make the most curious engines, or by deceiving others advance themselves, or that can subtly dispute the most curious niceties, or criticise upon the words of several languages; yet I will never call them wise, that are all that while the devil's slaves, the enemies of God, the refusers of grace, and are making haste to endless misery. And I think there is not one of those in hell who were once the subtle men on earth, that now take themselves to have been truly wise, or glory much in the remembrance of such wisdom.

And as the choice doth prove men wise, so the practice of this holy walking with God, doth make them much wiser than they were. As there must be some work of the Spirit to draw men to believe in Christ, and yet the Spirit is promised and given (in a special sort or measure) to them that do believe; so must there be some special wisdom to make men choose to walk with God; but much more is given to them in this holy course. As Solomon was wiser than most of the world, before he asked wisdom of God, or else he would not have made so wise a choice, and preferred wisdom before the riches and honours of the world; and yet it was a more notable degree of wisdom that was afterwards given him in answer to his prayers: so it is in this case.

There are many undeniable evidences to prove, that walking with God doth do more to make men truly wise, than all other learning or policy in the world.

1. He that walketh with God, doth begin aright, and settles upon a sure foundation; (and we use to say, that a work is half finished that is well begun;) he hath engaged himself to the best and wisest teacher; he is a disciple to him that knoweth all things. He hath taken in infallible principles, and taken them in their proper place and order; he hath learned those truths which will every one become a teacher to him, and help him to that which is yet unlearned. Whereas many that thought they were doctors in Israel, if ever they will be wise and happy, must "become fools (that is, such as they have esteemed fools) if ever they will be wise;" (1 Cor. iii. 18.); and must be called back with Nicodemus to learn Christ's cross, and to be taught that, "that which is born of the flesh is but flesh, and that which is born of the Spirit is Spirit;" and that therefore they "must be born again" (not only of water, but also of the Spirit) if ever they "will enter into the kingdom of heaven." (John iii. 3. 5, 6.) O miserable beginning, and miserable progress, when men that never soundly learned the mysteries of regeneration, and faith, and love, and self-denial, and mortification, do proceed to study names and words, and to turn over a multitude of books, to fill their brains with airy notions, and their common-places with such sayings as may be provision and furniture for their pride and ostentation, and ornament to their style and language; and know not yet what they must do to be saved, and indeed know nothing as they ought to know! (1 Cor. viii. 2.) As every science hath its principles, which are supposed in all the consequential verities; so hath religion as doctrinal and practical, those truths which must be first received, before any other can be received as it ought; and those things which must be first done, before any other can be done, so as to attain their ends. And these truths and duties are principally about God himself, and are

known and done effectually by those, and only those, that walk with God, or are devoted to him. It is a lamentable thing to see men immersed in serious studies, even till they grow aged, and to hear them seriously disputing and discoursing about the controversies or difficulties in theology, or inferior sciences, before ever they had any saving knowledge of God, or of the work of the Holy Ghost in the converting and sanctifying of the soul, or how to escape everlasting misery!

2. He that walketh with God hath fixed upon a right end, and is renewing his estimation and intention of it, and daily prosecuting it: and this is the first and greatest part of practical wisdom. When a man once knoweth his end aright, he may better judge of the aptitude and seasonableness of all the means. When we know once that heaven containeth the only felicity of man, it will direct us to heavenly thoughts, and to such spiritual means as are fitted to that end: if we have the right mark in our eye, we are more like to level at it, than if we mistake our mark. He is the wise man, and only he, that hath steadily fixed his eye upon that blessedness which he was created and redeemed for, and maketh straight towards it, and bends the powers of soul and body, by faithful, constant diligence to obtain it. He that hath rightly and resolvedly determined of his end, hath virtually resolved a thousand controversies that others are unsatisfied and erroneous in. He that is resolved, that his end is to please and glorify God, and to enjoy him forever, is easily resolved whether a holy life, or a sensual and worldly, be the way; whether the way be to be godly, or to make a mock at godliness: whether covetousness and riches, ambition and preferment, voluptuousness and fleshly pleasures, be the means to attain his end: whether it will be attained rather by the studying of the word of God, and meditating on it day and night, and by holy conference, and fervent prayer, and an obedient life; or by negligence, or worldliness, or drunkenness, or gluttony, or cards and dice, or beastly filthiness, or injustice and deceit. Know once but whither it is that we are going, and it is easy to know whether the saint, or the swine, or the swaggerer, be in the way. But a man that doth mistake his end, is out of his way at the first step; and the further he goes, the further he is from true felicity; and the more he erreth, and the further he hath to go back again, if ever he return. Everything that a man doth in the world, which is not for the right end (the heavenly felicity) is an act of foolishness and error, how splendid soever the matter or the name, may make it appear to ignorant men. Every word that an ungodly person speaketh, being not for a right end, is in him but sin and folly, however materially it may be an excellent and useful truth. While a miserable soul hath his back upon God, and his face upon the world, every step he goeth is an act of folly, and tending unto his further misery. It can be no act of wisdom, which tendeth to a man's damnation. When such a wretch begins to inquire and bethink him where he is, and whither he is going, and whither he should go, and to think of turning back to God, then, and never till then, he is beginning to come to himself, and to be wise. (Luke xv. 17.) Till God and glory be the end that he aimeth at, and seriously bends his study, heart and life to seek, though a man were searching into the mysteries of nature; though he were studying or discussing the notions of theology; though he were admired for his learning and wisdom by the world, and cried up as the Oracle of the earth, he is all the while but playing the fool, and going a more cleanly way to hell than the grosser sinners of the world! For is he wise, that knoweth not whether heaven or earth be better? Whether God or his flesh should be obeyed? Whether everlasting joys, or the transitory pleasures of sin should be preferred? Or that seemeth to be convinced of the truth in these and such like cases, and yet hath not the wit to make his choice, and bend

his life according to his conviction? He cannot be wise who practically mistakes his end.

3. He that walketh with God doth know those things with a deep, effectual, heart-changing knowledge, which other men know but superficially, by the halves, and as in a dream. And true wisdom consisteth in the intensiveness of the knowledge subjectively, as much as in the extensiveness of it objectively. To see a few things in a narrow room perspicuously and clearly, doth show a better eyesight, than in the open air to see many things obscurely, so as scarce to discern any of them aright; (like him that saw men walk like trees). The clearness and depth of knowledge, which makes it effectual to its proper use, is the greatness and excellency of it: therefore it is, that unlearned men that love and fear the Lord, may well be said to be incomparably more wise and knowing men than the most learned that are ungodly. As he hath more riches that hath a little gold or jewels, than he that hath many load of stones; so he that hath a deep, effectual knowledge of God the Father, and the Redeemer, and of the life to come, is wiser and more knowing than he that hath only a notional knowledge of the same things, and of a thousand more. A wicked man hath so much knowledge, as teacheth him to speak the same words of God, and Christ, and heaven, which a true believer speaks; but not so much as to work in him the same affections and choice, nor so much as to cause him to do the same work. As it is a far more excellent kind of knowledge which a man hath of any country by travel and habitation there, than that which cometh but by reading or report; or which a man hath of meat, of fruits, of wines, by eating and drinking, than that which another hath by hearsay: so is the inward heart-affecting knowledge of a true believer, more excellent than the flashy notions of the ungodly. Truth, simply as truth, is not the highest and most excellent object of the mind: but good, as good, must be apprehended by the understanding, and commended to the will, which entertaineth it with complacency, adhereth to it with choice and resolution, prosecuteth it with desire and endeavour, and enjoyeth it with delight. And though it be the understanding which apprehendeth it, yet it is the heart or will that relisheth it, and tasteth the greatest sweetness in it, working upon it with some mixture of internal sense, (which hath made some ascribe a knowledge of good, as such, unto the will). And it is the will's intention that causeth the understanding to be denominated practical: and therefore I may well say, that it is wisdom indeed when it reacheth to the heart. No man knoweth the truth of God so well as he that most firmly believeth him: and no man knoweth the goodness of God so well as he that loveth him most. No man knoweth his power and mercy so well as he that doth most confidently trust him: and no man knoweth his justice and dreadfulness so well as he that feareth him. No man knoweth or believeth the glory of heaven so well as he that most esteemeth, desireth and seeketh it, and hath the most heavenly heart and conversation. No man believeth in Jesus Christ so well, as he that giveth up himself unto him, with the greatest love, and thankfulness, and trust, and obedience. As James saith, "Show me thy faith by thy works," so say I, let me know the measure and value of my knowledge by my heart and life. That is wisdom indeed, which conformeth a man to God, and saveth his soul: this only will be owned as wisdom to eternity, when dreaming notions will prove but folly.

4. He that walketh with God hath an infallible rule, and taketh the right course to have the best acquaintance with it, and skill to use it. The doctrine that informeth him is divine: it is from heaven, and not of men: and therefore if God be wiser than man, he is able to make his disciples wisest; and teaching will more

certainly and powerfully illuminate. Many among men have pretended to infalli-bility, that never could justify their pretensions, but have confuted them by their own mistakes and crimes; but none can deny the infallibility of God. He never yet was deceived, or did deceive: he erreth not, nor teacheth error. Nicodemus knew Christ was to be believed, when he knew that he was "a teacher come from God." (John iii. 2.) Christ knew that the Jews themselves durst not deny the truths of John's doctrine, if he could but convince them that it was "from heaven, and not of men." It is impossible for God to lie: it is the devil that "was a liar from the beginning," and is yet the Father of lies. No wonder if they believe lies that follow such a teacher: and those that follow the flesh and the world, do follow the devil. They that will believe what their fleshly interests and lusts persuade them to believe, do believe what the devil persuadeth them to believe; for he persua-deth them by these, and for these. What marvel then, if there be found men in the world, that can believe that holiness is hypocrisy, or a needless thing? That those are the worst men that are most careful to please God! That the world is more worthy of their care and labour, than their salvation is! That the pleasures of sin for a season are more desirable, than the everlasting happiness of the saints! That cards and dice, and mirth and lust, and wealth and honour, are matters more delec-table than prayer, and meditating on the word of God, and loving him, and obey-ing him, and waiting in the hopes of life eternal! That gluttons and drunkards, and whoremongers, and covetous persons, may enter into the kingdom of God, &c. What wonder, if a thousand such damnable lies, are believed by the disciples of the father of lies? What wonder, if there are so many saint-haters and God-haters in the world, as to fill the earth with persecutions and cruelties, or make a scorn of that which God most highly valueth, and all this under pretences of order, or unity, or justice, or something that is good, and therefore fit to palliate their sin! Is there anything so false, or foul, or wicked, that Satan will not teach his followers? Is he grown modest, or moderate, or holy, or just? Is he reconciled to Christ, to Scripture, to godliness, or to the godly? Or is his kingdom of darkness at an end? And hath he lost the earth? Or are men therefore none of the servants of the devil, because they were baptized (as Simon Magus was) and call and think themselves the servants of Christ? As if still it were not the aft by which he gets and keeps disciples, to suffer them to wear the livery of Christ, and to use his name, that he may thus keep possession of them in peace, who else would be frighted from him, and fly to Christ! He will give them leave to study arts and sciences, and to understand things excellent of inferior use, so be it they will be deceived by him in the matters of God and their salvation. He can allow them to be learned lawyers, excellent physicians, philosophers, politicians, to be skillful artists, so be it they will follow him in sin to their damnation, and will overlook the "truth that should set them free." (John viii. 32.) Yea he will permit them (when there is no remedy) to study the holy Scriptures, if he may but be the expounder and applier of it. Yea he will permit them notionally to understand it, if they will not learn by it to be converted, to be holy, and to be saved. He can suffer them to be eminent divines, so they will not be serious Christians. Thus is the world by the grand deceiver buried in darkness to perdition, being "taken captive by him at his will." (2 Tim. ii. 26.) But the sanctified are all illuminated by the Holy Ghost, by whom their eyes are so effectually opened, that they "are turned from darkness unto light, and from the power of Satan unto God." (Acts xxvi. 18.) "The Father of glory hath given them the Spirit of wisdom and revelation, in the knowledge of Christ, that the eyes of their understanding being enlightened, they may know what is the hope of his calling, and what the riches of the glory of his inheritance in the saints." (Ephes. i. 17, 18.) Certainly that illumination of the Holy Ghost, which is so often mentioned in Scripture as given to all true believers, is not a fancy, nor an insignificant name: and if it signify anything, it signifieth somewhat that is much above the teaching of man. All that walk with God are taught of God! And can man teach like God? God hath access unto the heart, and there he doth transcribe his laws, and put them into our inward parts. And they that walk with him have not only his word to read, but his Spirit to help them to understand it: and being with him, in his family (yea, he dwelleth in them, and they in him) he is ready at hand to resolve their doubts: when he gave them his fear, he gave them the "beginning of wisdom." (Psal. cxi. 10.) He causeth them to "incline their ear to wisdom;" (Prov. ii. 2, 6.); and to "apply their hearts unto it;" (Psal. xc. 12.); "and maketh them to know it in the hidden parts." (Psal. li. 6.)

It is his law that they have determined to make their rule: they live as under his authority: they are more observant of his will and government, than of any laws or government of man. And as they obey man in and for the Lord, so they do it in subordination to him, and therefore not against him and his laws, which being the standard of justice, and the rule of rulers, and of subjects both, they are in the safest way of unerring wisdom, who walk with God according to that rule; and refuse to turn aside, though commanded by man, or enticed by Satan, the world, or flesh.

5. He that walketh with God is the most considerate person, and therefore hath great advantage to be wise. The frequent and serious thoughts of God, do awaken all the powers of the soul, so that drowsiness doth not hinder the understanding, and so occasion its deceit. There is scarce a more common and powerful cause of men's folly and delusion and perdition, in all the world, than that sleepiness and stupidity which hindereth reason from the vigorous performance of its office. In this senseless case, though a man both know and consider of the same truths, which in their nature are most powerful to cleanse and govern and save his soul, yet sluggishness doth enervate them: he knoweth them as if he knew them not, and considereth them as if he never thought of them. They work little more upon him, than if he believed them not, or had never heard of them. Even as a dream of the greatest matters, moveth not the sleeper from his pillow. In this senseless state, the devil can do almost anything with a sinner. He can make him sin against his knowledge: and when conscience hath frightened him into some kind of penitence, and made him cry out, 'I have sinned and done foolishly,' and caused him to promise to do so no more; yet doth the devil prevail with him to go on, and to break his promises, as if he had never been convinced of his sins, or confessed them, or seen any reason or necessity to amend: he doth but imprison the truth in unrighteousness, and bury it in a senseless heart: whereas if you could but awaken all the powers of his soul, to give this same truth its due entertainment, and take it deeper into his heart, it would make him even scorn the baits of sin, and see that the ungodly are beside themselves, and make him presently resolve and set upon a holy life. And hence it is, that sickness which causeth men to receive the sentence of death, doth usually make men bewail their former sinful lives, and marvel that they could be before so sottish as to resist such known and weighty truths: and it makes them purpose and promise reformation, and wish themselves in the case of those that they were wont before to deride and scorn: because now the truth is more deeply received and digested, by their awakened souls, and appeareth in its proper evidence and strength. There is no man but

must acknowledge that the same truth doth at one time command his soul, which at another time seems of little force. It is a wonder to observe how differently the same consideration worketh with a man when he is awakened, and when he is in a secure, stupid state.

Now this is his advantage that walks with God. He is much more frequently than others awakened to a serious apprehension of the things which he understandeth. The thoughts of the presence of the most holy God, will not suffer him to be secure and senseless as others are, or as he is himself, when he turneth aside from this heavenly conversation. He hath in God such exceeding transcendent excellencies, such greatness, such goodness continually to behold, that it keepeth his soul in a much more serious, lively frame than any other means could keep it in: so that whenever any truth or duty is presented to him, all his faculties are awake and ready to observe and improve it. A sermon, or a good book, or godly conference, or a mercy, when a man hath been with God in prayer and contemplation, will relish better with him, and sink much deeper, than at another time. Nay one serious thought of God himself, will do more to make a man truly and solidly wise, than all the reading and learning in the world, which shuts him out.

6. Walking with God doth fix the mind, and keep it from diversions and vagaries, and consequently much helpeth to make men wise. A straggling mind is empty and unfurnished. He that hath no dwelling, for the most part hath no wealth. Wandering is the beggar's life. Men do but bewilder and lose themselves, and not grow wise, whose thoughts are ranging in the corners of the earth, and are like masterless dogs, that run up and down according to their fancy, and may go any whither, but have business no where. The creature will not fix the soul; but God is the centre of all our thoughts: in him only they may unite, and fix, and rest. He is the only loadstone that can effectually attract and hold it steadfast to himself. Therefore he that walks with God is the most constant and unmoveable of men. Let prosperity or adversity come; let the world be turned upside down, and the mountains be hurled into the sea, yet he changeth not: let men allure or threat, let them scorn or rage, let laws, and customs, and governments, and interest change, he is still the same. For he knoweth that God is still the same, and that his word changeth not. Let that be death one year, which was the way to reputation another, and let the giddy world turn about as the seasons of the year, this changeth not his mind and life (though in things lawful he is of a yielding temper): for he knoweth that the interest of his soul doth not change with the humours or interests of men: he still feareth sinning, for he knoweth that judgment is still drawing on, in all changes and seasons whatsoever: he is still set upon the pleasing of the most holy God, whoever be uppermost among men; as knowing that the God whom he serveth is able to deliver him from man, but man is not able to deliver him from God. He still goeth on in the holy path, as knowing that heaven is as sure and as desirable as ever it was. "Surely he shall not be moved forever: the righteous shall be in everlasting remembrance. He shall not be afraid of evil tidings: his heart is fixed, trusting in the Lord: his heart is established, he shall not be afraid." (Psal. cxii. 6, 7.)

7. He that walketh with God, hath the great master-truths upon his heart, which are the standard of the rest, and the stock, as it were, out of which they spring. The great truths about God, and grace, and glory, have a greater power than many hundred truths of an inferior nature. And moreover, such a one is sure that he shall be wise in the greatest and most necessary points. He is guilty of no ignorance or error that shall keep him out of heaven, or hinder his acceptance

with his God. And if he be wise enough to please God and to be saved, he is wise indeed (as before was hinted).

8. Walking with God doth take off the vizor of deluding things, and keepeth us out of the reach and power of those objects and arguments which are the instruments of deceit. When a man hath been believingly and seriously with God, how easily can he see through the sophistry of the tempting world! How easily can he practically confute the reasonings of the flesh, and discern the dotage of the seeming subtleties of wicked men, that will needs think they have reason for that which is displeasing to their Maker, and tends to the damning of their souls! So far as a man is conversant with God, so far he is sensible, that all things are nothing, which can be offered as a price to hire him to sin: and that the name of preferment, and honour, and wealth, or of disgrace, and imprisonment, and death, are words almost of no signification, as to the tempter's ends, to draw the soul from God and duty. It is men that know not God, and know not what it is to walk with him, that think these words so big and powerful, to whom wealth and honour do signify more than God and heaven; and poverty, disgrace and death, do signify more than God's displeasure and everlasting punishment in hell. As it is easy to cheat a man that is far from the light, so is it easy to deceive the most learned man that is far from God.

9. Walking with God, doth greatly help us against the deceitful and erroneous disposition of our own hearts. The will hath a very great power upon the understanding: and therefore ungodly, fleshly men will very hardly receive any truth which crosseth the carnal interest or disposition: and will hardly let go any error that feedeth them; because their corrupted wills are a bias to their understandings, and make them desperately partial in all their reading and hearing, and hypocritical in their prayers and inquiries after truth. Interest and corruption locketh up their hearts from their own observation. Whereas a man that walketh with God, that is jealous, and holy, and just, and a searcher of the heart, is driven from hypocrisy, and forced to behave himself as in the open light, and to do all as in the sight of all the world, as knowing that the sight of God is of far greater concernment and regard. The partiality, corruption and bias of the heart, is detected and shamed by the presence of God. Therefore to walk with God is to walk in the light, and as children of the light, and not in darkness. And he that doth truth "cometh to the light, that his deeds might be manifest, that they are wrought in God: when everyone that doth evil hateth the light; neither cometh to the light lest his deeds should be reproved. And this is their condemnation, that light is come into the world, and men love the darkness rather than the light, because their deeds are evil." (John iii. 19-21.) It tendeth therefore exceedingly to make men wise, to walk with God, because it is a walking in the light, and in such a presence as most powerfully prevaileth against that hypocrisy, deceitfulness and partiality of the heart, which is the common cause of damning error.

10. Lastly, they that walk with God are entitled by many promises, to the guidance and direction of his Spirit. And blessed are those that have such a guide: at once a light in the world without them, and a light immediately from God within them. For so far as he is received and worketh in them, he will lead them into truth, and save them from deceit and folly, and having "guided them by his counsel, will afterwards take them unto glory." (Psal. lxxiii. 24.) Whereas the ungodly are led by the flesh, and often "given up to their own heart's lusts, to walk in their own counsels;" (Rom. viii. 1-13; Psal. lxxxi. 12;) till at last "the fools do say in their hearts, there is no God;" (Psal. xiv. 1.); "and they become corrupt and

abominable, eating up the people of the Lord as bread, and call not on his name:" (ver. 2. &c.): "Deceiving and being deceived: sensual, having not the Spirit;" (Jude 19.); "who shall receive the reward of their unrighteousness, as accounting it pleasure to riot in the day time." (2 Pet. ii. 13.)

IV. Another benefit of walking with God is, that it maketh men good, as well as wise. It is the most excellent means for the advancement of man's soul to the highest degree of holiness attainable in this life. If conversing with good men doth powerfully tend to make men good; conversing with God must needs be more effectual; which may appear in these particulars.

1. The apprehensions of the presence and attributes of God, do most effectually check the stirrings of corruption, and rebuke all the, vicious inclinations and motions of the soul: even the most secret sin of the heart, is rebuked by his presence, as well as the most open transgression of the life: for the thoughts of the heart are open to his view. All that is done before God, is done as in the open light: nothing of it can be hid: no sin can have the encouragement of secrecy to embolden it. It is all committed in the presence of the universal King and Lawgiver of the world, who hath forbidden it. It is done before him that most abhorreth it, and will never be reconciled to it. It is done before him that is the Judge of the world, and will shortly pass the sentence on us according to what we have done in the body. It standeth up in his presence who is of infinite majesty and perfection, and therefore most to be reverenced and honoured: and therefore if the presence of a wise, and grave, and venerable person will restrain men from sin, the presence of God apprehended seriously, will do it much more. It is committed before him who is our dearest friend, and tender Father, and chiefest Benefactor: and therefore ingenuity, gratitude and love will all rise up against it in those that walk with God. There is that in God, before the eyes of those that walk with him, which is most contrary to sin, and most powerful against it of anything in the world. Everyone will confess, that if men's eyes were opened to see the Lord in glory standing over them, it would be the most powerful means to restrain them from transgressing. The drunkard would not then venture upon his cups: the fornicator would have a cooling for his lusts: the swearer would be afraid to take his Maker's name in vain: the profane would scarce presume to scorn or persecute a holy life. And he that walketh with God, though he see him not corporally, yet seeth him by faith, and liveth as in his presence; and therefore must needs be restrained from sin, as having the means which is next to the sight of God. If pride should begin to stir in one that walks with God; O what a powerful remedy is at hand! How effectually would the presence of the great and holy God rebuke it and constrain us to say as Job xlii. 5, 6, "I have heard of thee by the hearing of the ear; but now mine eye seeth thee. Wherefore I abhor myself, and repent in dust and ashes." If worldly love, or carnal lust, should stir in such a one, how powerfully would the terrors of the Lord repress it; and his majesty rebuke it; and his love and goodness overcome it! If worldly cares or murmuring discontents begin to trouble such a one; how effectually will the goodness, the all-sufficiency and the faithfulness of God allay them, and quiet and satisfy the soul, and cause it to be offended at its own offence, and to chide itself for its repinings and distrust! If passion arise and begin to discompose us, how powerfully will the presence of God rebuke it, and the reverence of his majesty, and the sense of his authority and pardoning grace will assuage it, and shame us into silent quietness! Who dare let out his passions upon man, in the presence of his Maker, that apprehendeth his presence? The same I

might say of all other sins.

2. The presence and attributes of God apprehended by those that walk with him, is the potent remedy against temptations. Who will once turn an eye to the gold and glory of the world, that is offered him to allure to sin, if he see God stand by? Who would be tempted to lust or any sinful pleasure, if he observe the presence of the Lord? Satan can never come in so ill a time with his temptations, and have so little hope to speed, as when the soul is contemplating the attributes of God, or taken up in prayer with him, or any way apprehensive of his presence. The soul that faithfully walks with God, hath enough at hand in him to answer all temptations. And the further any man is from God, and the less he knoweth him, the more temptations can do upon him.

3. The presence of God affordeth the most powerful motives unto good, to those that walk with him. There is no grace in man, but is from God, and may find in God its proper object or incentive. As God is God, above the creature transcendently and infinitely in all perfections, so all the motives to goodness which are fetched from him, are transcendently above all that may be fetched from any creature. He that liveth always by the fire, or in the sunshine, is most like to be warm. He that is most with God, will be most like to God in holiness. Frequent and serious converse with him, doth most deeply imprint his communicable attributes on the heart, and make there the clearest impression of his image. Believers have learned by their own experience, that one hour's serious prayer, or meditation, in which they can get nigh to God in the Spirit, doth more advance their grace, than any help that the creature can afford them.

4. Moreover those that walk with God, have not only a powerful, but an universal incentive for the actuating and increasing of every grace. Knowledge, and faith, and fear, and love, and trust, and hope, and obedience, and zeal, and all have in God their proper objects and incentives. One creature may be useful to us in one thing, and another in another thing; but God is the most effectual mover of all his graces: and that in a holy harmony and order. Indeed he hath no greater motive to draw us to love him, and fear him, and trust him, and obey him, than himself. "It is life eternal to know him in his Son (John xvii. 3.) and that is, not only because it entitleth to life eternal, but also because it is the beginning and incentive of that life of holiness which will be eternal.

5. Moreover, those that walk with God, have a constant as well as a powerful and universal incentive to exercise and increase their graces. Other helps may be out of the way: their preachers may be silenced or removed: their friends may be scattered or taken from them: their books may be forbidden, or not at hand: but God is always ready and willing; they have leave at all times to come to him, and be welcome. Whenever they are willing they may go to him by prayer or contemplation, and find all in him which they can desire. If they want not hearts, they shall find no want of anything in God. At what time soever fear would torment them, they may draw near and put their trust in him. (Psal. lvi. 2-4; xi. 1; xviii. 2, 30; xxxi. 1, 6.) He will be a sure and speedy refuge for them, a very present help in trouble. (Psal. xlvi. 1; lxii. 7, 8; xci. 2, 9; xciv. 22.) Whenever coldness or lukewarmness would extinguish the work of grace, they may go to him, and find those streams of flaming love flow from him, those strong attractives, those wonderful mercies, those terrible judgments, of which, while they are musing, the fire may again wax hot within them. Psal. xxxix. 3.

6. Lastly, by way of encouraging reward, God useth to give abundantly of his grace, to those that walk most faithfully with him. He will show most love to

those that most love him. He will be nearest to them that most desirously draw nigh to him; while he forsaketh those that forsake him, and turneth away from those that turn away from him. "The hand of our God is for good upon all them that seek him; but his power and his wrath is against all them that forsake him." (2 Chron. xv. 2; Prov. i. 32; Ezra viii. 22.)

Thus it is apparent in all these evidences, that walking with God, is not only a discovery of the goodness that men have, but the only way to increase their grace, and make them better. O what a sweet humility, and seriousness, and spirituality appeareth in the conference, or conversation, or both, of those that newly come from a believing, close converse with God! When they that come from men and books, may have but a common mind or life. And those that come from the business and pleasure of the world and flesh, and from the company of foolish, riotous gallants, may come defiled, as the swine out of the mire!

V. Lastly to walk with God, is the best preparation for times of suffering, and for the day of death. As we must be judged according to what we have done in the body; so the nearer we find ourselves to judgment, the more we shall be constrained to judge ourselves according to what we have done, and shall the more perceive the effect upon our souls.

That this is so excellent a preparative for sufferings and death, will appear by the consideration of these particulars.

1. They that walk with God are most safe from all destructive sufferings; and shall have none but what are sanctified to their good. (Rom. viii. 28.) They are near to God, where destruction cometh not; as the chicken under the wings of the hen. They walk with him that will not lead them to perdition: that will not neglect them, nor sell them for naught, nor expose them to the will of men and devils, though he may suffer them to be tried for their good. No one can take them out of his hands. Be near to him, and you are safe: the destroyer cannot fetch you thence. He can fetch you (when the time is come) from the side of your merriest companions, and dearest friends; from the presence of the greatest princes; from the strongest tower, or most sumptuous palace, or from your heaps of riches, in your securest health: but he cannot take you from the arms of Christ, nor from under the wings of your Creator's love. "For there is no god like him, in heaven above, or on the earth beneath, who keepeth covenant and mercy with his servants, that walk before him with all their heart." (1 Kings viii. 23; xi. 38.) However we are used in our Father's presence, we are sure it shall be for good in the latter end: for he wanteth neither power nor love to deliver us, if he saw deliverance to be best.

2. Walking with God is the surest way to obtain a certainty of his special love, and of our salvation. And what an excellent preparative for sufferings or death such assurance is, I need not tell any considerate believer. How easy may it be to us to suffer poverty, disgrace or wrongs, or the pains of sickness or death, when once we are certain that we shall not suffer the pains of hell! How cheerfully may we go out of this troublesome world, and leave the greatest prosperity behind us, when we are sure to live in heaven forever! Even an infidel will say, that he could suffer or die, if he could but be certain to be glorified in heaven when he is dead!

3. Walking with God doth mortify the flesh, and all the affections and lusts thereof. The soul that is taken up with higher matters, and daily seeth things more excellent, becometh as dead to the things below: and thus it weaneth us from all that in the world which seemeth most desirable to carnal men. And when the flesh is mortified, and the world is nothing to us, or but as a dead or loathsome carcass, what is there left to be very troublesome in any suffering from the world? Or to

make us loath by death to leave it? It is men that know not God, that overvalue the profits and honours of the world; and men that never felt the comforts of communion with God, that set too much by the pleasures of the flesh: and it is men that set too much by these, that make so great a matter of suffering. It is he that basely overvalueth wealth, that whineth and repineth when he comes to poverty. It is he that sets too much by his honour, and being befooled by his pride, doth greatly esteem the thoughts or applauding words of men, that swelleth against those that disesteem him, and breaketh his heart when he falleth into disgrace. He that is cheated out of his wits by the pomp and splendor of a high and prosperous estate, doth think he is undone when he is brought low. But it is not so with him that walks with God: for being taken up with far higher things, he knoweth the vanity of these. As he seeth not in them anything that is worthy of his strong desires, so neither anything that is worthy of much lamentation when they are gone. He never thought that a shadow, or feather, or a blast of wind could make him happy: and he cannot think that the loss of these can make him miserable. He that is taken up with God, hath a higher interest and business, and findeth not himself so much concerned in the storms or calms that are here below, as others are, who know no better, and never minded higher things.

4. Walking with God doth much overcome the fear of man. The fear of him who can destroy both soul and body in hell fire, will extinguish the fear of them that can but kill the body. (Luke xii. 4.) The threats or frowns of a worm are inconsiderable to him that daily walketh with the great and dreadful God, and hath his power and word for his security. As Moses "esteemed the reproach of Christ greater riches than the treasures of Egypt, because he had respect to the recompense of reward; so he feared not the wrath of the king, for he endured as seeing him that is invisible." Heb. xi. 27.

5. Walking with God doth much prepare for sufferings and death, in that it breedeth quietness in the conscience. So that when all is at peace within, it will be easy to suffer anything from without. Though there is no proper merit in our works to comfort us, yet it is an unspeakable consolation to a slandered, persecuted man to be able to say, 'These evil sayings are spoken falsely of me, for the sake of Christ: and I suffer not as an evil doer, but as a Christian.' And it is matter of very great peace to a man that is hasting unto death, to be able to say as Hezekiah, "Remember now, O Lord, how I have walked before thee in truth, and with a perfect heart, and have done that which is good in thy sight." (2 Kings xx. 3.) And as Paul, 2 Tim. iv. 7, 8. "I have fought a good fight, I have finished my course, I have kept the faith; henceforth there is laid up for me a crown of righteousness," &c. And as 2 Cor. i. 12. "For our rejoicing is this, the testimony of our conscience, that in simplicity and godly sincerity, not with fleshly wisdom, but by the grace of God, we have had our conversation in the world." Such a testimony of conscience is a precious cordial to a suffering or a dying man. The time we have spent in a holy and heavenly conversation, will be exceedingly sweet in the last review, when time spent in sinful vanity, and idleness, and in worldly and fleshly designs, will be grievous and tormenting. The day is coming, and is even at hand, when those that are now the most hardened infidels, or obstinate, presumptuous sinners, or scornful, malicious enemies of holiness, would wish and wish a thousand times, that they had spent that life in a serious, obedient walking with God, which they spent in seeking worldly wealth, and laying up a treasure on earth, and feeding the inordinate desires of their flesh. I tell you, it is walking with God, that is the only way to have a sound and quiet conscience: and he that is healing and

settling his conscience upon the love of God and the grace of Christ, in the time of prosperity, is making the wisest preparation for adversity: and the preparation thus made so long before (perhaps twenty, or forty, or threescore years or more) is as truly useful and comfortable at a dying hour, as that part which is made immediately before. I know that besides this general preparation, there should be also a particular, special preparation for sufferings and death: but yet this general part is the chiefest and most necessary part. A man that hath walked in his life time with God, shall certainly be saved, though death surprise him unexpectedly, without any more particular preparation. But a particular preparation without either such a life, or such a heart as would cause it if he had recovered, is no sufficient preparation at all, and will not serve to any man's salvation. Alas! what a pitiful provision doth that man make for death and for salvation, who neglecteth his soul, despiseth the commands of God, and disregardeth the promises of eternal life, till he is ready to die, and then cryeth out, 'I repent, I am sorry for my sin, I would I had lived better:' and this only from the constraint of fear, without any such love to God and holiness which would make him walk with God if he should recover. What if the priest absolve this man from all his sins? Doth God therefore absolve him? Or shall he thus be saved? No, it is certain that all the sacraments and absolutions in the world will never serve to save such a soul, without that grace which must make it new and truly holy. The absolution of a minister of Christ, which is pronounced in his name, is a very great comfort to the truly penitent: for such God hath first pardoned by his general act of oblivion in the Gospel, and it is God that sendeth his messenger to them (in sacraments and ministerial absolution) with that pardon particularized and applied by themselves. But where the heart is not truly penitent and converted, that person is not pardoned by the Gospel, as being not in the covenant, or a child of promise; and therefore the pardon of a minister, being upon mistake, or to an unqualified person, can reach no further than to admit him into the esteem of men, and to the communion and outward privileges of the church (which is a poor comfort to a soul that must lie in hell): but it can never admit him into the kingdom of heaven. God indeed may approve the act of his ministers, if they go according to his rule, and deal in church administrations with those that make a credible profession of faith and holiness, as if they had true faith and holiness: but yet he will not therefore make such ministerial acts effectual to the saving of unbelieving or unholy souls. Nay (because I have found many sensual, ungodly people inclining to turn Papists, because with them they can have a quick and easy pardon of their sins, by the pope, or by the absolution of the priest) let me tell such, that if they understand what they do, even this cheat is too thin to quiet their defiled consciences: for even the Papist's school doctors do conclude, that when the priest absolveth an impenitent sinner, or one that is not qualified for pardon, such a one is not loosed or pardoned in heaven. (Leg. Martini de Ripalda Exposit. Liber. Magist. lib. 4. dist. 18. p. 654, 655, and p. 663, 664, dist. 20. Aquin. dist. 20. q. 1. a. 5. Suar. Tom. 4. in 3. p. disp. 52. Greg. Valent. Tom. 4. disp. 7. q. 20. p. 5. Tolet. lib. 6. cap. 27. Navar. Notab. 17. and 18. Cordub. de indulg. lib. 5. q. 23.) They deny not the truth of those words of Origen. Hom. 14. ad cap. 24. Levit. 'Exit quis a fide, perexit de castris Ecclesiaer etiamsi, Episcopi voce non abjiciatur: sicut contra interdum fit, at aliquis non recto judicio eorum qui praesunt Ecclesiae, foras mittatur: sed si non egit ut mereretur exire, nihil laeditur: interdum enim quod foras mittitur, intus est; et qui foris est, intus videtur retineri.' And what he saith of excommunication, is true of absolution: an erring key doth neither lock out of heaven, nor let into heaven. A godly believer shall be saved though the priest condemn him: and an unbeliever or ungodly person shall be condemned by God, though he be absolved by the priest.

Nay, if you have not walked with God in the Spirit, but walked after the flesh, though your repentance should be sound and true at the last, it will yet very hardly serve to comfort you, though it may serve to your salvation: because you will very hardly get any assurance that it is sincere. It is dangerous lest it should prove but the effect of fear (which will not save) when it cometh not till death do fright you to it. As, Augustine saith, 'Nullus expectet, quando peccare non potest: arbitrii enim libertatem quaerit Deus, ut deleri possint commissa; non necessitatem, sed charitatem, non tantum timorem: quia non in solo timore vivit homo.' Therefore the same Augustine saith, 'Siquis positus in ultima necessitate voluerit accipere poenitentiam, et accipit; fateor vobis, non illi negamus quod petit; sed non praesumimus quod bene hinc exit: si securus hinc exierit, ego nescio. Poenitentiam dare possumus, securitatem non possumus.' You see then how much it is needful to the peace of conscience at the hour of death, that you walk with God in the time of life.

6. Moreover, to walk with God is an excellent preparation for sufferings and death, because it tendeth to acquaint the soul with God, and to embolden it both to go to him in prayer, and to trust on him, and expect salvation from him. He that walketh with God is so much used to holy prayer, that he is a man of prayer, and is skilled in it; and hath tried what prayer can do with God: so that in the hour of his extremity, he is not to seek either for a God to pray to, or a Mediator to intercede for him, or a Spirit of adoption to enable him as a child to fly for help to his reconciled Father. And having not only been frequently with God, but frequently entertained and accepted by him, and had his prayers heard and granted, it is a great encouragement to an afflicted soul in the hour of distress, to go to such a God for help. And it is a dreadful thing when a soul is ready to go out of the world, to have no comfortable knowledge of God, or skill to pray to him, or encouragement to expect acceptance with him: to think that he must presently appear before a God whom he never knew, nor heartily loved, being never acquainted with that communion with him in the way of grace, which is the way to communion in glory; O what a terrible thought is this! But how comfortable is it when the soul can say, 'I know whom I have believed. The God that afflicteth me is he that loveth me, and hath manifested his love to me by his daily attractive, assisting and accepting grace. I am going by death to see him intuitively, whom I have often seen by the eye of faith, and to live with him in heaven, with whom I lived here on earth: from whom, and through whom, and to whom was my life! I go not to an enemy, nor an utter stranger, but to that God who was the spring, the ruler, the guide, the strength and the comfort of my life! He hath heard me so oft, that I cannot think he will now reject me. He hath so often comforted my soul, that I will not believe he will now thrust me into hell. He hath mercifully received me so oft, that I cannot believe he will now refuse me. Those that come to him in the way of grace, I have found he will in no wise cast out.' As strangeness to God doth fill the soul with distrustful fears, so walking with him doth breed that humble confidence, which is a wonderful comfort in the hour of distress, and a happy preparation to sufferings and death.

7. Lastly, to walk with God, doth increase the love of God in the soul, which is the heavenly tincture, and inclineth it to look upward, and being weary of a sinful flesh and world, to desire to be perfected with God. How happy a preparation for death is this, when it is but the passage to that God with whom we desire

to be, and to that place where we fain would dwell forever! To love the state and place that we are going to, being made connatural and suitable thereto, will much overcome the fears of death. But for a soul that is acquainted with nothing but this life, and savoureth nothing but earth and flesh, and hath no connaturality with the things above, for such a soul to be surprised with the tidings of death, alas! how dreadful must it be.

And thus I have showed you the benefits that come by walking with God, which if you love yourselves with a rational love, methinks should resolve every impartial, considerate reader, to give up himself without delay, to so desirable a course of life. Or, if he have begun it, to follow it more cheerfully and faithfully than he had done.

Chapter VII.

I am next to show you that believers have special obligations to this holy course of life, and therefore are doubly faulty if they neglect it: though indeed, to neglect it totally, or in the main drift of their lives, is a thing inconsistent with a living faith.

Consider, 1. If you are true Christians, your relations engage you to walk with God. Is he not your reconciled Father, and you his children in a special sense? And whom should children dwell with, but with their Father? You were glad when he received you into his covenant that he would enter into so near a relation to you, as he expresseth, (2 Cor. vi. 17, 18.) "I will receive you, and will be a Father to you, and ye shall be my sons and daughters, saith the Lord Almighty." And do you draw back, as if you repented of your covenant; and were not only weary of the duty, but of the privileges and benefits of your relation? You may have access to God when others are shut out: your prayers may be heard, when the prayers of the wicked are abominable: you may be welcome, when the worldlings, and ambitious, and carnal are despised. He that dwelleth in the highest heaven, is willing to look to you with respect, and "dwell with you, when he beholdeth the proud afar off." (Isa. lxvi. 1, 2; lvii. 15, 16.) And yet will you not come that may be welcome? Doth he put such a difference between you and others, as to feed you as children at his table, while others are called dogs, and are without the doors, and have but your crumbs and leavings? And yet will you be so foolish and unthankful, as to run out of your Father's presence, and choose to be without among the dogs? How came your Father's presence to be so grievous to you and the privileges of his family to seem so vile? Is it not some unchildlike carriage the guilt of some disobedience or contempt that hath first caused this? Or have you fallen again in love with fleshly pleasures, and some vanity of the world? Or have you had enough of God and godliness, till you begin to grow weary of him? If so, you never truly knew him. However it be, if you grow as indifferent to God, do not wonder if shortly you find him set as light by you. And believe it, the day is not far off, in which the Fatherly relation of God, and the privileges of children, will be more esteemed by you: when all things else forsake you in your last distress, you will be loath that God should then forsake you, or seem as a stranger to hide his face. Then you will cry out, as the afflicted church, "Look down from heaven, and behold from the habitation of thy holiness and of thy glory. Where is thy zeal and thy strength? The sounding of thy bowels, and of thy mercies towards me? Are they restrained? Doubtless thou art our Father: though Abraham be ignorant of us, and Israel acknowledge us not, thou, O Lord, art our Father, our Redeemer, thy name is from everlasting." (Isa. lxiii. 15, 16.) Nothing but God, and his Fatherly relation will then support you. Attend him therefore, and with reverent, obedient cheerfulness and delight, converse with him as with your dearest Father. For since the beginning of the world, men have not known by sensible evidence, either of the ear or the eye, "besides God himself, what he hath prepared for him that waiteth for him." Isa. lxiv. 4. Though he be "wroth with us because we have sinned, yet doth he meet him that rejoiceth and worketh righteousness, that remembereth him in his ways;" (Ver. 5.) Say not, I have played abroad so long that I dare not now go home. I have sinned so greatly, that I dare not speak to him, or look him in the face. Come yet but with a penitent, returning heart, and thou mayest be accepted through the Prince of Peace. Prodigals find better entertainment than they did expect, when once they do but resolve for home. If he allow us to begin with "Our Father which art in heaven," we may boldly proceed to ask forgiveness of our trespasses, and whatever else is truly good for us. But, alas, as our iniquities seduce us away from God, so the guilt of them affrighteth some from returning to him, and the love of them corrupteth the hearts of others, and makes them too indifferent as to their communion with him; so that too many of his children live as if they did not know their Father, or had forgotten him. We may say as Isa. lxiv. 6-9. "But we are all as an unclean thing, and all our righteousnesses are as filthy rags, and we all do fade as a leaf, and our iniquities like the wind have taken us away: and there is none that calleth upon thy name, that stirreth up himself to take hold of thee; for thou hast hid thy face from us, and hast consumed us because of our iniquities: but now, O Lord, thou art our Father; we are the clay, and thou our potter, and we are all the work of thy hand. Be not wroth very sore, O Lord, neither remember iniquity forever. Behold, see, we beseech thee, we are all thy people." O do not provoke your Father to disown you, or to withdraw his help, or hide his face, or to send the rod to call you home! For if you do, you will wish you had known the privileges of his presence, and had kept nearer to him! Be not so unnatural, so unthankful, so unkind, as to be weary of your Father's presence, (and such a Father's too) and to take more delight in any others.

Moreover you are related to God in Christ, as a wife unto a husband, as to covenant union, and nearness and dearness of affection, and as to his tender care of you for your good: and is it seemly, is it wisely or gratefully done of you, to desire rather the company of others, and delight in creatures more than him? (Isa. liv. 5, 6.) How affectionately doth thy Maker call himself the Husband of his people! And can thy heart commit adultery, and forsake him? "My covenant they broke, though I was a Husband to them, saith the Lord." (Jer. xxxi. 32.) O put not God to exercise; his jealousy. It is one of his terrible attributes, to be "a jealous God." And can he be otherwise to thee, when thou lovest not his converse or company, and carest not how long thou art from him in the world? Woe to thee if he once say as Hos. ii. 2. "She is not my wife, neither am I her husband."

Nay; more than this, if you are Christians, you are members of the body of Christ; and therefore how can you withdraw yourselves from him, and not feel the pain and torment of so sore a wound or dislocation? You cannot live without a constant dependence on him; and communication from him: "I am the true Vine, and my Father is the Husbandman: abide in me, and I in you.—I am the Vine, ye are the branches; he that abideth in me, and I in him, the same bringeth forth much fruit; for without me, ye can do nothing. If ye abide in me, and my words abide in you, ye shall ask what ye will, and it shall be done unto you." (John xv. 1, 4, 5.)

So near are you to Christ, that he delighteth to acquaint you with his secrets. O how many mysteries doth he reveal to those that walk with him, which carnal strangers never know, mysteries of wisdom, mysteries of love and saving grace, mysteries of Scripture, and mysteries of Providence, mysteries felt by inward experience, and mysteries revealed, foreseen by faith! Not only the strangers that pass by the doors, but even the common servants of the family, are unacquainted with the secret operations of the Spirit, and entertainments of grace, and joy in believing, which those that walk with God either do or may possess. Therefore Christ calleth you friends, as being more than servants. "Ye are my friends, if ye do whatsoever I command you: henceforth I call you not servants; for the servant knoweth not what his Lord doth: but I call you friends; for all things that I have heard of my Father, I have made known unto you." (John xv. 14, 15.) It is true, for all this, that every true Christian hath reason (and is apt) to complain of his darkness and distance from God. Alas! they know so little of him, and of the mysteries of his love and kingdom, that sometimes they are apt to think that they are indeed but utter strangers to him; but this is, because there is infinitely more still unknown to them than they know! What! Can the silly shallow creature comprehend his infinite Creator? Or shall we know all that is to be known in heaven, before we enjoy all that is to be enjoyed in heaven? It is no more wonder to hear a believer pant and mourn after a fuller knowledge of God, and nearer access to him, than to seek after heaven, where this will be his happiness. But yet, though his knowledge of God be small, compared with his ignorance, that little knowledge of God which he hath attained, is more mysterious, sublime and excellent, than all the learning of the greatest unsanctified scholars in the world. Walk with him according to the nearness of your relations to him, and you shall have this excellent knowledge of his mysteries, which no books or teachers alone can give. You shall be effectually touched at the heart with the truths which others do uneffectually hear: you shall be powerfully moved, when they are but uneffectually exhorted. When they only hear the voice without them, you shall hear the voice within you, and as it were behind you, saying, This is the way, walk in it. O that you could duly value such a friend, to watch over you, and for you, and dwell in you, and tell you faithfully of every danger, and of every duty, and teach you to know good and evil, and what to choose, and what to refuse! How closely and delightfully would you converse with such a blessed friend, if you rightly valued him!

2. Moreover, you that are the servants of God, have by your covenant and profession, renounced and forsaken all things else (as they stand in any opposition to him, or competition with him) and have resigned yourselves wholly unto him alone; and therefore with him must you converse, and be employed, unless you will forsake your covenant. You knew first that it was your interest to forsake the world and to turn to God; you knew the world would not serve your turn, nor be instead of God to you, either in life, or at death; and upon this knowledge it was that you changed your master, and changed your minds, and changed your way, your work, your hopes. And do you dream now that you were mistaken? Do you begin to think that the world is fitter to be your God or happiness? If not, you must still confess that both your interest and your covenant do oblige you to turn your hearts and minds from the things which you have renounced, and to walk with him that you have taken for your God, and to obey him whom you have taken for your King and Judge, and to keep close to him with purest love, whom you have taken for your everlasting portion. Mark what you are minding all the day, while you are neglecting God; is it not something that you have renounced? And did not you renounce it upon sufficient cause? Was it not a work of your most serious deliberation? And of as great wisdom, as any that ever you performed? If it were, turn not back in your hearts again from God unto the renounced creature. You have had many a lightning from heaven into your understandings, to bring you to see the difference between them; you have had many a teaching, and many a warning, and many a striving of the Spirit, before you were prevailed with to renounce the world, the flesh and the devil, and to give up yourself entirely and

absolutely to God. Nay, did it not cost you the smart of some afflictions, before you would be made so wise? And did it not cost you many a gripe of conscience, and many a terrible thought of hell, and of the wrath of God, before you would be heartily engaged to him, in his covenant? And will you now live as strangely and neglectfully towards him, as if those days were quite forgotten? And as if you had never felt such things? And as if you had never been so convinced, or resolved? O Christians, take heed of forgetting your former case, your former thoughts, your former convictions, and complaints, and covenants! God did not work all that upon your hearts to be forgotten; he intended not only your present change, but your after remembrance of it, for your close adhering to him while you live; and for your quickening and constant perseverance to the end. The forgetting of their former miseries, and the workings of God upon their hearts in their conversion, is a great cause of mutability and revolting, and of unspeakable hurt to many a soul.

Nay, may you not remember also what sorrow you had in the day of your repentance, for your forsaking and neglecting God so long? And will you grow again neglective of him? Was it then so heinous a sin in your eyes? And is it now grown less? Could you then aggravate it so many ways (and justly), and now do you justify or extenuate it? Were you then ready to sink under the burden of it? And were so hardly persuaded that it would be forgiven you? And now do you make so small a matter of it? Did you then so much wonder at your folly, that could so long let out your thoughts and affections upon the creature, while you neglected God and heaven? And do you begin to look that way again? Do you now grow familiar with a life so like to that which was once your state of death, and bear that easily that once was the breaking of your heart? O Christians, turn not away from that God again, who once fetched you home, with so much smart and so much grace, with such a twist of love and fatherly severity! Methinks when you remember how you were once awakened, you should not easily fall asleep again. And when you remember the thoughts which then were in your hearts, and the tears that were in your eyes, and the earnest prayers which you then put up, that God would receive, and take you for his own, you should not now forget him, and live as if you could live without him. Remember that so far as you withdraw your hearts from God, and let them follow inferior things, so far you contradict his works upon your hearts, so far you violate your covenant with him, or sin against it; so far you are revolters, and go against the principal part of your professed religion; yea, so far you are ungodly as you thus withdraw your hearts from God. Cleave to him, and prosecute your covenant, if you will have the saving benefits of his love and covenant.

3. Moreover, the servants of God are doubly obliged to walk with him, because they have had that experience of goodness, the safety and sweetness of it, which strangers have not. Do you not remember how glad you were, when you first believed that he pardoned and accepted you, and how much you rejoiced in his love and entertainment, and how much better you found your Fathers house, than ever you had found your sinful state, and how much sweeter his service was, than you did before believe? It is like you can remember something like that which is described in Luke xv. 20, 22-24, "And he arose and came to his father; but when he was yet a great way off, his father saw him, and had compassion, and ran and fell on his neck and kissed him: and the son said unto him, Father, I have sinned against heaven, and in thy sight, and am no more worthy to be called thy son. But the father said to his servants, Bring forth the best robe and put it on him, and put a ring on his hand, and shoes on his feet, and bring hither the fatted

calf, and kill it, and let us eat and be merry; for this my son was dead, and is alive again, he was lost, and is found." What would you have thought or said of this prodigal, if after all this, he should have been weary of his father's house and company, and have taken more pleasure in his former company? Would you not have said, He was a forgetful and unthankful wretch, and worthy never more to be received? I do not speak to you now as to apostates, that are turned ungodly, and have quite forsaken God and holiness; but I beseech you consider what it is, after such experiences and obligations as these, so much as to abate your love, and grow remiss, and mindless, and indifferent, as if you were weary of God, and were inclined to neglect him, and look again to the world for your hope, and satisfaction, and delight! As you love your souls, and as you would avoid the sorrows which are greater than any that ever you felt, take heed of slighting the love that hath done such wonders for you, and of dealing so unthankfully with the everlasting God, and of turning thus away from him that hath received you! Remember, whilst you live, the love of your espousals. Was God so good to you at first, and holiness so desirable, and is it not so still?

And I am sure that your own experience will bear witness, that since that time, in all your lives, it never was so well with you as when you walked most faithfully with God. If you have received any falls and hurts, it hath been when you have straggled from him; if ever you had safety, peace or joy, it hath been when you have been nearest to him; your wounds, and grief, and death, hath been the fruit of your own ways, and of your forsaking him: your recovery, and health, and life, have been the fruit of his ways, and of your adhering to him: many and many a time you have confessed this, and have said, It is good for me to draw near to God. He hath helped you when none else could help you; and comforted you when none else could comfort you. How far are you above the worldling's happiness, when you are nigh to God! One lively thought of his greatness, and excellency, and of his love to you in Jesus Christ, will make the name of wealth, and honour, and favour, and preferment, and sensual pleasures, to seem to you as words of no signification. How indifferent will you be, as to your prosperity in the world, when you feel what it is to walk with God! If you are lively, experimental Christians, you have found this to be true: have you not found that it is the very health and ease, and proper employment of your souls to walk with God, and keep close to him, and that all goes well with you while you can do thus, however the world doth esteem or use you, and that when you grow strange or disobedient to God, and mindless of his goodness, his presence and his authority, you are like the stomach that is sick, and like a bone that is out of joint, that can have no ease till it be healed, and restored to its proper place? No meats or drinks, no company nor recreation, no wealth or greatness will serve to make a sick man well, or ease the dislocated bones. Nothing will serve a faithful, holy soul but God; this is the cause of the dolour of his heart, and of the secret groans and complainings of his life, because in this life of distance and imperfection, he finds himself so far from God; and when he hath done all that he can, he is still so dark, and strange, and cold in his affections! When persecution driveth him from the ordinances and public worship, or when sin hath set him at a greater distance from his God, he bemoaneth his soul, as David in his banishment from the tabernacle: "As the hart panteth after the water-brooks, so panteth my soul after thee, O God. My soul thirsteth for God, for the living God; when shall I come and appear before God? My tears have been my meat day and night, while they continually say unto me, Where is thy God?" (Psal. xlii. 1, 2, &c.) And it is no wonder, if with his greatest joy, he be yet clouded with these sorrows, because he yet wanteth more of God than he enjoyeth; and his enjoying graces (love and joy) are yet imperfect. But when he hath attained his nearest approach to God, he will have fullness of delight in fullness of fruition.

O Christians! do I need to tell you, that after all the trials you have made in the world, you have never found any state of life that was worthy your desires, nor that gave you any true content, but only this living upon God? If you have not found such comfort here as others have done, yet at least you have seen it afar off, within your reach; as men that in the Indies, in the discovery of plantations, expect gold mines, when they find those golden sands that promise it. You have found a life which is certainly desirable, and leadeth to joy in the midst of sorrow; and it is no small joy to have a certain promise and prospect of everlasting joy. It is therefore more excusable in those that never tasted any better than the pleasures of the flesh, to neglect this sweeter heavenly life, than it is in you, that have been convinced by your own experience, that there is no life to be compared with it.

4. Your walking with God is the necessary prosecution of your choice and hopes of life eternal. It is your necessary preparation to your enjoying him in heaven. And have you fixed on those hopes with so great reason and deliberation, and will you now draw back and be slack in the prosecution of them? Have you gone so far in the way to heaven, and do you now begin to look behind you, as if you were about to change your mind? Paul setteth you a better example: "Yea doubtless, I account all things but loss, for the excellency of the knowledge of Christ Jesus, my Lord; for whom I have suffered the loss of all things, and do count them but dung, that I may win Christ, and be found in him—If by any means I might attain to the resurrection of the dead; not as though I had already attained, either were already perfect; but I follow after, if that I may apprehend that for which also I am apprehended of Christ Jesus: brethren, I count not myself to have apprehended, but this one thing I do, forgetting those things which are behind, and reaching forth unto those things which are before, I press towards the mark for the prize of the high calling of God in Christ Jesus." (Phil. iii. 8-13.) He compareth himself to a runner in a race, that till he apprehend the prize or mark, doth still make forward with all his might, and will not so much as mind or look at anything behind him, that would turn him back, or stop him in his course. The world and the flesh are the things behind us: we turned our backs upon them at our conversion, when we turned to God: it is these that would now call back our thoughts, and corrupt our affections, when we should run on, and reach forward to the heavenly prize: it is God and heaven, and the remaining duties of a holy life, that are the things before us! And shall we now look back? What we, that are running and striving for a crown of endless glory! We, that if we lose it, do lose our souls and hopes forever! We, that have loitered in the morning of our lives, and lost so much precious time as we have done! We, that have gone so far in our way, and held out through so many difficulties and assaults! Shall we now grow weary of walking with God, and begin to look to the things behind us? Did he not tell us at the first, that father and mother, and house and land, and life, and all things must be forsaken for Christ, if we will be his disciples? These are the things behind us, which we turned our back on when we consented to the covenant; and are they now grown better? Or is God grown worse, that we turn our hearts from him to them? When we first begun our Christian race, it was upon supposition that it was for that immortal crown, which all the world is not to be compared to: and have we not still the same consideration before us, to move us to hold on till we

attain it? Hold on Christians, it is for heaven; is there not enough in that word to drive back all the cares and pleasures, that importune your minds to forget your God? Is there not enough in that word to quicken you up in your greatest dullness and to call you home, when you are wandering from God; and to make you again fall out with all that would seduce you, or divert you, and call it vanity and vexation of spirit? Methinks the forethought of that life and work which you hope to have with God for ever, should make you earnestly desire to have as much of the like on earth, as is here to be attained! If it will be your heaven and happiness then, it must needs be desirable now. It is not beseeming a man that saith he is seeking for perfect communion with God in heaven, and that above all things, (as every Christian doth) to live in a daily neglect or forgetfulness of God on earth. Delightfully to draw near him, and exercise all our faculties upon him, or for him, sometimes in prayer and contemplation on himself, and always in works of obedience to him; this is the life that beseemeth those that profess to seek eternal life. O therefore let us make it our daily work, to keep our God and glory in our eye, and to spur on our dull affections, and in the diligent attendance and following the Captain of our salvation, to prosecute our expected end.

5. Lastly consider, that God doth purposely provide you hard entertainment in the world, and cause every creature to deny you the pleasure and satisfaction which you desire, that so you may have none to walk with but himself, with any heart-settling comfort and content. If you see not enough in him to allure you to himself, you shall feel enough in the world to drive you to him: if his love and goodness will not serve you alone to make him your pleasure, and hold you to him in the best, and most excellent way (of love), at least the storms and troubles that are abroad shall show you a necessity of keeping close to God; and the love of yourselves shall help you to do that, which was not done by the attraction of his love alone. If you will put him to it, to send out his command to every creature, to cross and vex you, and disappoint all expectations from it, that so he may force you to remember your Father and your home, deny not then but it is long of yourselves that you were not saved in an easy way. Would you wish God to make that condition pleasant to you, which he seeth you take too much pleasure in already (or seek and desire it, at least), when as it is the pleasantness of the creature that is your danger, and which detaineth your thoughts and affections from himself? If you could but learn to walk with him, and to take up your pleasure in his love appearing to you in his creatures, and to make their sweetness a means to your apprehension of the sweetness of his favour, and of the everlasting joys, then you might say the creature doth you good; and then it is like you might be permitted to possess and use it for such pleasure. The jealous God will watch your hearts, though you watch them not; and he will make you know that he seeth which way they run out from him, and what creature it is that is minded and delighted in, while he is neglected, as if he were unsuitable, and scarce desirable. And you must never look that he should long permit you those prohibited delights, or let you alone in those idolatrous inclinations. If he love you, he will cure that carnal love, and recover your love to himself that hath deserved it. If he intended not your salvation, he may let you go, and try again whether the creature will prove better to you than himself; but you cannot think that he will thus let go his children that must live with him forever. Have you not perceived that this is the design and meaning of his afflicting and disappointing providences, even to leave you no comfortable entertainment or converse but with himself, and with his servants, and with those means that lead you to himself? If you begin to desire to lodge

abroad in strange habitations, he will uncover those houses, and will not leave you a room that is dry to put your head in; or he will throw open the doors, and leave all open to the lust of ravenous beasts and robbers. He will have thy heart, and he will have thy company, because thou art his child, and because he loveth thee. He will allow thee neither thy carnal delights nor hopes. If he perceive thee either taking that pleasure in thy prosperity, which thou shouldest take in him alone, or hoping at least that the world may hereafter prove more amiable and delightful to thee; the more he loveth thee, the more his providence shall conspire with his grace, to change thy mind, by depriving thee of thy unwholesome, dangerous delights, and of all thy hopes of such hereafter. Use the world as a traveller, for the ends to which it was ordained, to the service of God, and the furtherance of thy salvation, and then thou shalt find that God will furnish thee with all that is necessary to these necessary ends: but if the world must have your love and care, and must be your chiefest business and delight, and your excuse for not attending upon God, murmur not, nor marvel not, if he dispose of it and you accordingly. If you are yet too healthful to think with seriousness on your eternal state; if you are too rich to part with all for Christ, or openly to own his cause; if you are too much esteemed in the world to own a scorned, slandered religion; if you are so busy for earth, that you cannot have time, to think of heaven; if you have so much delight in house or land, or in your employment, or recreations, or friends, that God and godliness can have little or none of your delight: marvel not then if God do shake your health, or waste your riches, or turn your honour into contempt, and suffer men to slander and reproach you, and spit in your face, and make you of no reputation: marvel not if he turn you out of all, or turn all to your grief and trouble, and make the world a desert to you, and the inhabitants as wolves and bears. The great lesson that Christ hath undertaken to teach you, is the difference betwixt the Creator and the creature, and the difference betwixt heaven and earth. The great work that Christ hath undertaken to do upon you, is to recover your hearts from the world to God: and this lesson he will teach you, and this work he will do upon you, whatever it cost you: for it must be done. Yet is not the world unjust enough, or cruel, or vexatious enough to you, to teach you to come home, and take up your content and rest in God? It may then prove more cruel, and more vexatious to you, till you have better learned this necessary lesson. Yet is not your condition empty enough of carnal delusory pleasures, to wean you from the world, and make you look to surer things? Yet are you keeping up your worldly hopes, that the world will again prove better to you, and that you shall have happy days hereafter? It seems you are not yet brought low enough: you must yet take another purge, and perhaps a sharper than you took before: you must have more bloodletting, till your deliration cease, and your feverish thirst after creature comforts do abate. It is sad that we should be so foolish and unkind, as to stay from God, as long as any preferments, or pleasures, or profits in the world, will entertain us: but seeing it is so, let us be thankful both to that grace and that Providence which cureth us. If you perceive it not better to dwell with God, than with a flattering, prospering world, he will try whether you can think it better to dwell with God, than with a malicious, cruel, persecuting world: and whether it be better to have your hearts in heaven, than in poverty, prison, banishment or reproach. If you find it not better to converse with God, than with those that honour you, please you, or prefer you; he will try whether you can think it better to converse with him, than with those that hate, revile, belie, and persecute you. And are these the wise and wholesome methods of our great Physician? And shall we not rather be ruled by him, than by our brutish appetites, and think better of his counsels, than of the blind concupiscence of the flesh? Let this be the issue of all our sufferings, and all the cruelties and injuries of the world, to drive us home to converse with God, and to turn our desires, and labours, and expectations, to the true felicity that never will forsake us; and then, the will of the Lord be done! Let him choose his means, if this may be the end: let us kiss the rod, and not revile it, if this may be the fruit of his corrections. Who will not pray that God would deny us those contents, which keep us from seeking our content in him? And that he would deny us all those hurtful pleasures which hinder us from pleasing him, or from making him and his ways our chiefest pleasure, and that he would permit us no such creature-converse, as hindereth our converse with him? It is best living there (be it in prison or at liberty) where we may live best to God. Come home, O suffering Christian, to thy God! Take up thy content and rest in him; be satisfied with him as thy portion; and remember where it is that he is to be fully and perpetually enjoyed; and then it is good for thee that thou wast afflicted; for all thy sufferings have their end.

Printed in Great Britain
by Amazon